D1327705

# THE STORY OF
# L. M. MONTGOMERY

# L. M. MONTGOMERY BOOKS
## IN ORDER OF FIRST PUBLICATION

L. M. MONTGOMERY IN 1904

# THE STORY OF

# *L. M. Montgomery*

by
HILDA M. RIDLEY

GEORGE G. HARRAP & CO. LTD

LONDON  TORONTO  WELLINGTON  SYDNEY

*First published in Great Britain* 1956
by GEORGE G. HARRAP & CO. LTD
182 High Holborn, London, W.C.1

*Composed in Bell type and printed by
Western Printing Services Ltd, Bristol
Made in Great Britain*

# FOREWORD

"Anne," declared Bliss Carman, the well-known Canadian poet, in a review of L. M. Montgomery's first novel, "is one of the immortal children of fiction." Mark Twain pronounced her "the sweetest creation of child life yet written." She takes her place with Little Nell, Tiny Tim, Peter Pan, Alice, of the Wonderland and the Looking Glass, Heidi, Topsy, Maggie Tulliver, and Oliver Twist. For the teen-ager Anne is a loved confidante, sharing her sensitive, wondering explorations of the mysteries of life. Anne's secret dreams and longings are hers, hers are Anne's. "I love the Anne Books," said a tall High School girl. "I read them over and over. There's nothing else like them."

Seldom has a first novel received the acclaim of *Anne of Green Gables*. As Miss Ridley tells us, "Grey-haired men and women, Supreme Court justices and heads of households were moved to laughter or tears" by the quaint sayings of this unforgettable child. The book soon went into many impressions, and was translated into Dutch, Danish, Swedish, French, Spanish, and

Polish. Eventually it was printed in Braille. Letters came to the author not only from children but from "soldiers in India, missionaries in China, traders in Africa, monks in far-away monasteries, and from trappers in the Canadian North."

L. M. Montgomery draws strength and beauty from Nature, in all her moods and circumstances. Her descriptions of the familiar background of her Prince Edward Island childhood have poetic beauty and pantheistic insight. The recent increased demand for more wholesome reading shows the truth of the words of Queen Elizabeth's 1954 Christmas broadcast: "The upward course of the nation's history is due in the long run to the soundness of heart of its average men and women." Books are often the outcome of the cultural, intellectual, and emotional climate of the author's childhood. So also the character of a child is profoundly influenced by the books which first open magic casements over seas, perilous or faery.

It is interesting to assess how far any novel is autobiographical. L. M. Montgomery certainly set her tales against the familiar background of her own early life. She does, indeed, show us her created characters through the lens of her personal vision and associations. But, like Jane

Austen, she kept within the range of her experience, and so never failed to obtain results.

Miss Ridley's purpose in this biography has been to present something of the background of L. M. Montgomery's youth and creative period, so that we might see how her character developed, and trace to its source the spring from which poured the waters of this fresh, inspiring, creative literary stream. "There are so many Annes in me," she once wrote. And in nearly all her stories there is a strong autobiographical content.

Lucy Maud Montgomery was born shortly after *Little Women* appeared. Until the publication of *Anne of Green Gables* in 1908, Louisa Alcott had no rivals in her chosen field. But with the Anne series literary observers realized that a new planet had swum into their ken. From the earliest days of the human race, grown-ups and children have listened wide-eyed to a good story-teller. And what a story-teller L. M. Montgomery is! Her tales are as fresh and imaginative as a spring morning. Besides an interesting plot, the enthralled teen-ager delights in the high spirits, the healthy humour, and the darting fancy of creative writing which seems designed especially for youth.

The public will warmly welcome a biography

which brings the author of the Anne novels very close to us. As Sir Arthur Quiller-Couch once said, "Like most human instincts, that which prompts us to be curious concerning the lives of great authors, as of other great men, is healthy enough if temperately controlled. Literature being so personal a thing, you cannot understand it until you have some personal conception of the one who wrote it." Miss Ridley has combined painstaking research with a special flair for sensing L. M. Montgomery's intellectual and spiritual qualities.

M. M. MITCHELL

# ACKNOWLEDGMENTS

MY sincere thanks are due to the following relatives and friends of the late Mrs Ewan Macdonald (L. M. Montgomery):

Mrs George Campbell and her son, James Townsend Campbell, of Park Hill, Prince Edward Island, to whom I am indebted for the use of "The Alpine Path," a sketch of her own life, which L. M. Montgomery contributed in 1917 to *Everywoman's World*, of Toronto, and for other valuable information.

Chester Cameron Macdonald, Q.C., of Toronto, who told me something about the life of his mother in Leaskdale, Norval, and Toronto, and who furnished most of the photographs which illustrate this book.

Mrs R. E. Mutch, of Charlottetown, Prince Edward Island, lifelong friend of L. M. Montgomery.

Miss Jean Gill, Librarian of the Legislative and Public Library of Charlottetown.

Mrs Harlan Found, of Charlottetown, whose summer cottage is the house at Clifton where L. M. Montgomery was born.

Mrs R. J. Austin, of Kingston, Ontario, who nursed Mrs Ewan Macdonald at Leaskdale Manse when her second son, Stuart, was born.

Mrs J. A. McClintock and Mrs Mark Weldon, of Uxbridge, Ontario, members of The Hypatia Club, of which Mrs Ewan Macdonald was for several years the Honorary President.

Mrs J. E. Mustard, of Uxbridge, Ontario, who was a member of the Presbyterian Church at Leaskdale, Ontario, when the Rev. Ewan Macdonald was pastor.

Mrs R. F. Willis, of Uxbridge, a good friend of the Macdonald family.

Mrs D. C. MacGregor (Marian Keith), who knew L. M. Montgomery well when she lived at Leaskdale, Norval, and Toronto.

H.M.R.

# CONTENTS

# ILLUSTRATIONS

# I

## A WRITER'S BACKGROUND

On cold winter evenings, when the fireside drew the members of her family together, little Lucy Maud Montgomery loved to listen to the tales told by her elders as they recalled old times. She thrilled to the romance of stories which showed how the lure of adventure had driven her forefathers westward from the old land—often known to men and women whose parents were Canadian born and bred as 'Home.'

To Lucy Maud, Prince Edward Island, the little province in which she had been born (in 1874), was home. She loved its red soil, and the glimpses of the sea she caught at every turn of a winding road. Has it not been named by the Indians who first occupied it Abegweit, which meant "The Home Cradled on the Waves"? Gradually she began to form some clear conception of just how her ancestors had arrived in this tiny, sea-encircled province only a hundred and forty miles in length, a province set in the blue waters of the Gulf of St Lawrence, north-east of New Brunswick and north of Nova Scotia, and, although so small, the one in which the "Fathers of Confederation" had met in 1864 for a preliminary conference which led to the union of the Canadian provinces.

To this island had come, many years before, Lucy Maud's great-great-grandfather, Hugh Montgomery, who had sailed from Scotland on a vessel bound for Quebec. Her grandfather chuckled as he told the story.

"He'd never have settled here at all if it hadn't been for the caprices of a woman's will," he explained. "You see, his wife, poor soul, was desperately sea-sick throughout the long voyage across the Atlantic. When the ship reached the north shore of Prince Edward Island the captain stopped it and sent a boat ashore for water to replenish his supply. Feeling sorry for Mrs Montgomery, he told her she might go along in the boat for a little change. She went all right, but no sooner had she set foot on dry land than she vowed nothing would drive her off it again. In vain her husband pleaded with her, expostulated, and argued; she wouldn't budge! And so at last he had to give in to her. And that's how the Montgomerys came to settle in Prince Edward Island, instead of in Quebec."[1]

[1] There were three Montgomery brothers who set sail from Scotland in a vessel bound for Quebec. Hugh

Another story of those early days concerned Hugh Montgomery's son, Donald, Lucy Maud's great-grandfather. At Richmond Bay, near Cavendish, Prince Edward Island, lived the Penmans. George Penman, a United Empire Loyalist, had been a Paymaster in the British Army, but when he came to Canada from the United States at the close of the War of Independence, having forfeited all his property, he was very poor. So beautiful were his daughters, Nancy and Betsey, however, that they had many suitors. One of them was Donald Montgomery.

"So smitten with Nancy was young Donald," related Lucy Maud's grandfather, "that he made the best of what he had on hand for courting her. One day he hitched a half-broken steer to a rude old wood sled and hied him over to Richmond Bay to propose to her."

---

Montgomery settled in Prince Edward Island. Another brother, after landing, took the next boat back to Scotland. What became of the third? Not until many years later did L. M. Montgomery learn. In an address she made before a club at Thornhill, Ontario, she stressed the fact that no one knew the fate of this brother. After the meeting a lady approached her and said, "I can tell you what happened to the third brother. He settled in York County, in the Eglinton Avenue area, and one of his descendants operated Montgomery's Tavern, the scene of the Mackenzie Rebellion of 1837."

B

In spite of this somewhat uncouth approach, he was accepted, and a happy marriage ensued. The son of Donald and Nancy became well known as Senator Montgomery, who inherited his striking good looks from his mother. He married his first cousin, the daughter of Nancy's sister, Betsey, who had married David Murray.

"So you see Nancy and Betsey were both your great-grandmothers," Lucy Maud was reminded at this point. "Betsey mightn't have been as beautiful as her sister, but she had very advanced views on women, so advanced that it was she who took the initiative in the courting of David, and proposed to him! She must have known what she was about, because the marriage that followed was called one of the happiest in the world."

Of her mother's family—the Macneills—Lucy heard stories just as interesting. Some of these concerned the literary talents of many of the members of this side of the family. Her great-great-grandfather, John Macneill, came to Prince Edward Island in 1775 from Argyllshire, where his family had espoused the lost cause of the Stuarts. He settled on a north-shore farm at Cavendish, and had a family of twelve children. His cousin, Hector Macneill, was a minor Scottish poet, and author of several well-known lyrics, among them "Saw ye my wee thing, saw ye my ain thing," "I lo'ed ne'er a laddie but one," and "Come under my plaidie," often erroneously attributed to Burns.

William Macneill, Lucy Maud's great-grandfather, was the oldest of John Macneill's twelve children. Considered a very clever and well-educated man for those times, he was commonly known as "Old Speaker Macneill," and he exercised a beneficial influence in provincial politics. He married Eliza Townsend, whose father was Captain John Townsend, of the British Navy. James Townsend, the Captain's father, had received from George III a grant of land in Prince Edward Island which he called Park Corner, after the family estate in England. Hopefully he set forth to claim his portion, bringing with him across the Atlantic his wife, Elizabeth, an Englishwoman who proved herself to be almost as stubborn as the Scottish wife of Hugh Montgomery.

"Bitterly homesick she was—rebelliously so," Grandmother Macneill told Lucy Maud. "For weeks after her arrival at Park Corner she wouldn't take off her bonnet, but walked the floor in it, demanding to be taken home."

"But, Grandma, what did she do at nights?" inquired Lucy Maud. "Did she take it off when she went to bed and put it on again in the morning?"

Grandmother pursed her lips. "She must have slept in it, if she slept at all. But anyway, the day came when she realized it was impossible for her husband to take her home, so at last she took off her bonnet and resigned herself to her fate."

Lucy Maud liked to visit the old family graveyard at Park Corner, where in a sequestered spot sleep Elizabeth Townsend and her husband. On a worn red sandstone slab which marks the grave the following epitaph appears:

*To the memory of James Townsend, of Park Corner, Prince Edward Island. Also of Elizabeth, his wife. They emigrated from England to this Island, A.D. 1775, with two sons and three daughters, viz., John, James, Eliza, Rachel and Mary. Their son John died in Antigua in the life time of his parents. His afflicted mother followed him into Eternity with patient resignation on the seventeenth day of April, 1795, in the 69th year of her age. And her disconsolate husband departed this life on the 25th day of December, 1796, in the 87th year of his age.*

William and Eliza Macneill (*née* Townsend) had a large family. Although their education was somewhat scanty, due to the conditions of those rude pioneer days, when there were only occasional terms at the district schools, all the children had marked intellectual ability. Lucy Maud's grandfather, Alexander Macneill, had strong literary leanings, and could write good prose. His brothers, William and James, were poets who composed satirical, witty, and dramatic verse.

One of young Lucy Maud's joys was to hear her grandfather recite the poems of his brothers. James was especially gifted, and had composed hundreds of poems which were never written down. With the advantages of a good education, this farmer in a remote part of Prince Edward Island might have become renowned. A sister, Lucy Maud's great-aunt, Mary Lawson, was a born *raconteur*. The child never wearied of her stories. A woman of keen intelligence, and with a remarkable memory, she was a strong formative influence in the little girl's life. Lucy Maud listened with eager interest to Aunt Mary's stories of her girlhood and of the sayings and doings of the folk who had contributed to the development of her island home. They made an indelible impression on her sensitive mind, and formed part of a storehouse of memories upon which in later years she drew to good advantage.

## II

## A SOLITARY CHILD

*I chanced to see at break of day*
*The solitary child.*

Wordsworth

Sometimes on those winter evenings when her grandparents told stories around the family hearth Lucy Maud thought wistfully of two absent ones—her mother and her father. Ever since early infancy she had lived in the home of her mother's parents, the Macneills, in their farm-house at Cavendish, a settlement on the north shore of Prince Edward Island, eleven miles from a railway and twenty-four miles from the nearest town. Her birthplace had been near-by Clifton, where her parents had lived for the first year of their marriage. But after the birth of Lucy Maud illness overtook her young mother, Clara Woolner Macneill, and she longed for the old family homestead, surrounded by apple orchards, in which she had been born. Yielding to her nostalgic craving for her mother and home, her husband moved his family to Cavendish, where—when Lucy Maud was yet only twenty-one months old—she died in the surroundings familiar to her from childhood.

Lucy Maud was a solitary child, given to day-dreaming and imaginative fancies. The loss of her mother and the departure of her father soon afterwards to a business post in Prince Albert, Saskatchewan, threw her much on her own resources. As she had no child companions, she invented some for herself. In the sitting-room of the Macneill farm stood a big book-case used as a china cabinet. A large oval glass in each door dimly reflected the objects in the room. When she stared at her reflection in the mirror of the left-hand door she saw, not herself, but a little girl of her own age whom she called Katie Maurice. She loved Katie dearly, and used to prattle to her by the hour, giving and receiving confidences. Of the reflection in the right-hand door she was not as fond. It belonged to one who was always very sad, and prone to tell her dismal stories of her troubles. This reflection she called Lucy Gray, and she tried to give her as much attention as she gave Katie, lest her feelings be hurt. There they lived, Katie and Lucy, in the fairy room behind the book-case.

The earliest memory of Lucy Maud's childhood went back to the day when she saw her mother lying in her coffin. She had been too young at the time to feel any real sorrow at her loss, but as she grew older she became conscious of a vacuum in her life. Sometimes at twilight, when the fire in the sitting-room cast light and flickering shadows on the walls, she used to commune about her sense of loss with her bookcase friends.

"I remember seeing her in her coffin. . . . Father was standing by it, holding me in his arms. I wore a little white muslin dress, and Father was crying. Grown-ups were seated around the room, and they looked sadly at Father and me, and whispered together. Behind them the window was open, and green vines were trailing across it, making shadows dance over the floor in a pool of sunshine. . . ."

"And how did your mother look?" asked Katie Maurice.

"She looked sweet, although her face was thin and worn as if she had suffered a good deal. People used to say she was very pretty, and she still looked pretty as she lay there. Her hair was a lovely golden-brown, and she had long lashes that brushed her cheeks. . . . Why was Mother so still? And why was Father crying? I put out my hand and laid it against Mother's cheek. It was so cold it scared me."

"Poor little Lucy!" whispered Lucy Gray, sympathetically.

"That's what I heard the grown-ups say. Then Father drew me back into his arms and tried to comfort me. Soon he carried me from the room, and I never saw her again."

Where was her mother? Her father told her that she had gone to Heaven. But where was Heaven, her active little brain inquired.

One Sunday, when she could not have been more than four years old, her Aunt Emily took her to the old church at Clifton, the village where she had been born. The minister in his sermon mentioned Heaven, that strange, mysterious place about which Lucy Maud knew so little.

"Aunt Emily, where's Heaven?" she whispered.

To whisper in church was considered an unpardonable sin. Aunt Emily did not commit it. Without a word, she gravely pointed upward. The little girl, gazing in the same direction, saw a small, square hole in the ceiling of the old church, just at the place where her aunt pointed. She took it for granted that her mother must be in the portion of the church above the ceiling. Why couldn't she and her aunt go up through the hole and see her? She resolved that when she grew bigger she would go to Clifton and find some means of getting up into Heaven and finding her mother.

She told her book-case friends about her discovery of Heaven. Even when communing with them, little Lucy Maud expressed herself in careful English. She was in many ways a precocious child. By the age of three she had mastered the alphabet, and she could not remember the time when reading had not seemed as natural to her as the capacity for breathing and eating.

But besides reading and converse with her book-case friends, Lucy Maud possessed an inborn love of nature. Just as she had discerned the beauty in her dead mother's face, so she caught the fugitive loveliness of the wayside flower, the pale beauty of a tall birch as the moonlight fell upon it, or the charm of a fern growing in a quiet dell. Every apple-tree in the orchard that surrounded the Macneill farm had for her an individuality, and she called each by name. There was "Aunt Emily's tree," "Uncle Leander's tree," the "Little Syrup tree," the "Spider tree," and so on.

With such resources, arising out of unusual attributes, the childhood of Lucy Maud could not be called unhappy. All the same, her good Grandmother Macneill sometimes felt uneasy about

the little girl's propensities. Very practical herself, the spectacle of her granddaughter in the
twilight talking to unseen presences—"for all
the world as if they were right in the room with
her"—seemed to her, to put it mildly, "un-
natural."

"Perhaps it isn't good for her to be so much
alone," she confided to her daughter, Lucy's
Aunt Emily, a pretty, lively girl who was 'keeping company' with a young man of the district.

"Well, Mother, I'll soon be getting married,
and then perhaps you could take in some children
to board," suggested Emily.

Grandmother Macneill kept that thought in
mind.

# III

## JUDGMENT SUNDAY

At Park Corner, not very far from the Macneill farm, lived Senator Montgomery, Lucy Maud's grandfather. He and his family resided in what was then known as the Old House, a quaint and delightful dwelling, with many cupboards and nooks and little unexpected flights of stairs that stirred a sense of mystery in Lucy Maud. In her early years she often paid visits there, and was always sure of a good time. She was a favourite with the servants in the kitchen, and much enjoyed watching their activities, and tasting the pie or pudding the cook was preparing. Amid the novelty of such surroundings she lost much of her dreaminess, and the cook used to declare that she was "wide-awake and full of ginger."

But it was here, when she was about five years old, that she had the most serious illness of her life—an attack of typhoid fever. She was sitting in front of the stove, watching the cook 'riddling' the fire with a long bar of iron, when it occurred to her that it would be fun to do some 'riddling' herself. She watched her opportunity, and when the cook put down the bar she seized it—but at the wrong end! As a result her hand was terribly burned. It was Lucy Maud's first initiation into physical pain—or, at least, the first one that she could remember—and she suffered horribly, and cried bitterly. Her howls brought her grand-parents and aunts to the scene. Roundly the Senator scolded the cook for her carelessness, while the women lost no time in applying remedies of various kinds to the badly burned hand and arm of the child.

Even in her pain, Lucy Maud found some satis-faction in the commotion she had caused. For the time being she felt herself to be more important than she had ever been before. At last she cried herself to sleep, with her hand and arm thrust into a pail of ice-cold water, the only device that seemed to give her any relief.

The next morning she awoke with a violent headache, and as the day advanced it grew worse. In a few days the doctor pronounced her illness to be typhoid fever. Several times her condition became so low that nobody thought she could possibly recover. Her Grandmother Macneill was sent for, and at length, under her ministra-tions, Lucy Maud took a turn for the better.

In those days convalescents were not dieted as strictly as they are to-day, and the first solid meal

Lucy Maud enjoyed—long before she was able to leave her bed—consisted of rich, home-made fried sausages. By all the rules, such a meal should have killed her or given her a serious set-back. It did neither. Lucy Maud, who was very hungry, ate the sausages ravenously, and felt no ill results. In fact, not very long afterwards, she was able to return home with her grand-mother.

Pensive and quiet after her illness, she continued to hold soliloquies with herself, or to commune with her book-case friends and, as the summer advanced, to find happiness in nature. But one June day she heard Grandmother Macneill read an item from the newspaper that filled her with dismay. The beautiful earth, with its blossoms and sunshine which she loved so much, was to end on the following Sunday. Lucy Maud had a naïve faith in the truth of the printed word, perhaps because she had derived so much pleasure from it, and she wondered how her grandmother and her Aunt Emily could take the momentous news so calmly.

"Grandma, doesn't it say in the Bible that on the last day the trumpet will sound and the dead arise from their graves?"

"Yes, the Good Book does say that, child," Grandmother Macneill replied, rather absently.

She was busy preparing a substantial meal, and had forgotten the newspaper item in question.

"But it will be terrible to see the dead arising, after lying so long in the earth, Grandma! How will they look, do you think?"

Grandmother Macneill grunted. "That I can't say."

"And the earth will have big cracks in it, and the trees and flowers will be burned up, and the birds will die!" Lucy Maud's voice ended in a wail.

"What are you talking about, child? You let your fancy run away with you!" Grandmother's voice was a little impatient. "Run away. Can't you see I'm busy?"

On the Saturday before the fateful Sunday Lucy Maud knew hardly a moment's respite from terror.

"Aunt Emily, will you go to Sunday School to-morrow afternoon?" she inquired.

"Of course. Why not?"

"But didn't you hear what Grandma read in the paper about the last day being to-morrow?" she insisted.

Aunt Emily only laughed. Her matter-of-fact behaviour gave Lucy Maud some comfort, but then, she thought again, had not the forecast of what was to happen on the following day been *printed*? That night sleep was out of the question for her. Might not the last trump sound at any moment? She kept her bedroom door wide open, so that she could hear the gentle breathing of her grandmother, punctuated by an occasional snore from her grandfather. The grown-ups, she reflected, didn't seem to worry at all about the impending end of the world.

Sunday dawned. Birds sang in the trees outside her window, pale sunlight glanced into her room. Lucy Maud arose and hurried into her clothes. Before the last trump sounded, she must see again all the beloved objects that the garden held—the pansy bed, the "bleeding hearts," and the gay and many-coloured tulips.

Breezes from the south blew to meet her. She saw the shadows of the spruces, long and clear-cut. Never had the skies looked more exquisite, or the flowers and trees fresher. Could God put an end to all this? Her conception of His goodness warred with her hitherto implicit faith in the printed word.

At breakfast she listened to the talk of the grown-ups.

"Look at the child!" exclaimed Grandfather Macneill. "She's so pale she looks as if she hadn't slept a wink all night."

"Why, don't you know she believes the end of

the world's coming to-day?" giggled Aunt Emily. "Come, Maud, you'd better eat your porridge. It may be your last meal."

"Don't tease her, Emily!" Grandfather Macneill spoke seriously. "I'd forgotten about that newspaper item. The Good Book says the last day may come as a thief in the night, so how do we know it may not end to-day?"

"Well, in my day," declared Grandmother Macneill, "I've heard tell of the end of the world coming three different times! Old Peter Johnson was so sure of it, twenty years ago, that he gave away his farm and had his faithful dog shot—all to be ready for what never happened!"

The bright morning sped away. In the afternoon Aunt Emily went as usual to Sunday School. Lucy Maud studied the pictures in *The Pilgrim's Progress*. Even though there might be a mistake about the exact time of the end of the world, she was determined to be prepared.

At length the long day came to an end, and, as the descending sun stained the purple sky-line of the Gulf, Lucy Maud drew a deep breath of relief. It really looked as if the beautiful green world of blossoms and trees that she loved so much were to last for a while longer.

Very sensitive, she did not like being teased, and she was thankful when her grandparents and

C

her aunt refrained from saying anything further about "Judgment Sunday." But another trial was in store for her. An old man came to visit the Macneills. He was amiable, but rather mischievous, and he won Lucy Maud's undying hatred by calling her "Johnny" every time he spoke to her. In vain, with childish rage, she protested against this insult. Her anger amused the old gentleman hugely, and incited him to persist in using the objectionable name. When the time came for him to go away, she refused to shake hands with him. This caused him to laugh uproariously. "Oh, well, I won't call you 'Johnny' any more," he conceded. "After this I'll call you 'Sammy.'"

To the old man (as to many other adults) the teasing of a touchy child was just fun; but to Lucy Maud—and in this she was not unlike other children—it was the poison of asps. She never afterwards heard the mention of this old man's name without a deep feeling of resentment.

# IV

## SCHOOL-DAYS

The time came for Lucy Maud to go to school. She was six years old, and her Grandmother Macneill thought it would do her good to mix with other children. The Cavendish school-house, a white-washed, low-eaved building, was not far from the Macneill farm-house. It stood near a spruce grove, which, with its winding paths, ferns, mosses, and broad brook, was one of Lucy Maud's favourite haunts.

She was taken to school on the first day by her Aunt Emily, who left her in the charge of some of the "big girls"—pupils who seemed all but grown up to Lucy, as they were ten years old. Nothing eventful happened on that day, but on the second Lucy Maud, having overslept, was late, and had to go to school alone. Bashfully she slipped into a seat beside a 'big girl,' and the next moment was dumbfounded to hear a peal of laughter from the children around her. *She had entered the room with her hat on.* Her humiliation and shame on discovering this oversight made her feel like sinking through the floor. She snatched at the offending article, but was told by the teacher to go and put it in its proper place. It was a very crushed morsel of humanity who crept away to do as she was told.

Unaccustomed to mixing with children of her own age, Lucy Maud was painfully conscious of any differences between herself and them. She noticed that all the other pupils went to school barefooted, while she herself was obliged to wear buttoned boots. Those buttoned boots became a grievance to her, and she pleaded with her grandmother to let her go without them, but in vain. It was not until some time later that she learned from a school-mate how much she was envied by the other girls for her "lovely buttoned boots."

Her grandmother also insisted that she wear at school the good, serviceable aprons which she had made for her. These aprons were long, sack-like garments, with *sleeves*. No one in the school had ever worn aprons like them. Once Lucy Maud heard one of the girls sneeringly describe them as "baby aprons," and her shame was intense.

"Couldn't the sleeves be cut off?" she asked her grandmother.

"Certainly not!" replied that strong-minded lady.

Another point of difference between her and

the other pupils was that many of them lived so far away from the school that they had to bring their lunches with them. Lucy Maud envied them, because at noon they sat in sociable rings on the playground, or in groups under trees, while she had to return home for a good hot dinner. Great was her delight when on a few stormy winter days her grandmother packed a lunch for her to eat at the school. She felt then that she was 'one of the crowd.'

Gradually, however, six-year-old Lucy Maud began to take her place among the children. She did sums with them, learned the multiplication table, wrote 'copies,' read lessons, and took part in spelling exercises. She was in the second book of the old Royal Reader series. At home she had gone through the primer, with its cat and rat definitions, and then had gone into the Second Reader, thus skipping the First Reader. She always mourned the missing of this First Reader, but writing and reading came so easily to her that the loss did not affect her standing.

After she had been going to school for a year, she became aware of an impending change at the Macneill farmhouse. Her Aunt Emily, always dear to her, seemed strangely elated, and the young man with whom she 'kept company' appeared on the scene more frequently than ever.

She was not surprised to learn that her aunt was very soon to be married.

Great preparations for the wedding were made. For weeks before it actually took place the kitchen was the centre of importance. There was much baking, frosting and decoration of cakes, and cooking of special food for the occasion. The wedding was one of the good old-fashioned kind. It took place at seven o'clock in the evening, and was followed by a big supper at which all the relatives on both sides of the Macneill family were present. This meant that practically everybody in the community was at the table. Cavendish had been settled in 1790 by three Scottish families—the Macneills, Simpsons, and Clarks. These families had intermarried to such an extent that only those born and bred in Cavendish knew whom it was safe to criticize, or to omit from an invitation to a wedding.

Lucy Maud remembered that she had once heard her Aunt Mary Lawson remark that "the Macneills and Simpsons always considered themselves a little better than the common run," and she had repeated a rather ill-natured local saying sometimes cast by outsiders at the original settlers of Cavendish: "From the conceit of the Simpsons, the pride of the Macneills, and the vainglory of the Clarks, good Lord deliver us."

Among those present at the supper, Lucy Maud could not detect any special evidences of conceit, pride, or arrogance. A spirit of utmost good-fellowship prevailed. Games and dancing followed the supper, and at one o'clock another big meal was served. Through all the proceedings Lucy Maud contrived to keep awake. Probably because there was no vacant place in which to put her to bed, she was allowed to remain up with her elders.

But as the time drew near when she knew that she must part from her beloved aunt a feeling of resentment overcame her. Approaching her new uncle, she pounded him with her little fists, exclaiming, "I *hate* you for taking away my Aunt Emily!"

Between excitement and too much indulgence in good things she became ill, and was laid up for a week following the wedding festivities.

## V

## COMRADES

Now that Aunt Emily was gone Grandmother Macneill thought it might be advisable, for Lucy Maud's sake, to take in some children to board. In the following summer two little boys became residents of the farm-house. Their names were Wellington and Nelson, but they were known to Lucy Maud as Well and Dave. Wellington was just her own age, and Dave a year younger. What fun those three children had during the next three years! In the summer they gardened, picnicked, and climbed trees, and in the long winter evenings they played games around the fire. They knew the joy of building their own playhouse in the spruce grove near the farm. To them the door they manufactured for the house, consisting of rough boards nailed uncertainly together, and a trifle rickety, was as fair as the Gate Beautiful of the Temple of the Jews, just because they had made it themselves. They had a little garden of their own in which they grew vegetables and flowers, rejoicing when some hardy sunflowers thrust their heads above the soil, or a few beans sprouted.

To Lucy Maud the boys were tremendous assets, because their characters and pursuits opened up new fields for her eager mind to explore. Even at an early age, she tended to be selective in her affections, recognizing from the first those who were likely to be kindred spirits, and these boys proved to be after her own heart. Both were gifted with imagination, and she was thrilled to discover that they believed in the existence of ghosts.

At first Lucy Maud was inclined to be sceptical about the validity of some of the stories the boys told her, but under the spell of their implicit faith she herself became infected.

A typical story was the one told by Well when he and Lucy were perched on the steps of the back porch of their home on a summer afternoon.

"My grandma," he related in his serious way, "went out one evening to milk the cows, and saw my grandpa come out of the house, drive the cows into the yard, and then go down the lane. Grandma was puzzled, because Grandpa was sick, and she'd ordered him to lie down on the sofa. She hurried back into the house, intending to scold him for not doing as he was told, and to her surprise she saw that he was lying on the sofa just as she had left him, and he'd never left the house at all! So it must have been his wraith that drove the cows. What else could it be?"

Finding that their ordinary haunts were too commonplace for the entertainment of ghosts, the children picked out a certain spruce grove in the field below the farm orchard, and decided to people it with creatures of their own fancy. At first they only pretended that they saw 'white things' flitting through the grove, but soon they began to believe in their own myths, and not one of them would have been brave enough to go near the grove after sunset.

One evening Dave ran out of the farm-house to find Lucy Maud in the apple orchard.

"There's a bell ringing inside!" he exclaimed, with popping eyes, "and every one's out, so who can it be?"

"What kind of a bell, Dave?" asked Lucy Maud.

"Like nothing ever heard before! It's a ghostly one, I'm sure."

The children decided to wait for the return of their elders before venturing again into the house. When Grandfather Macneill heard about the strange bell, he laughed.

"I gave the old clock in the kitchen a good cleaning this afternoon," he explained, "and it

L. M. MONTGOMERY'S GREAT-AUNT, MARY LAWSON, TO WHOM
SHE WAS INDEBTED FOR MANY OF THE TALES SHE WOVE INTO HER
BOOKS

L. M. Montgomery, aged Twenty-three

seemed to do her good, for she started striking the hours, something she hasn't done for years. What you heard, Dave, must have been eight o'clock striking!"

Another story the boys told was about a dissipated youth going home in the wee sma' hours of Sunday from some orgy, and being pursued by a lamb of fire, with its head cut off and hanging by a strip of skin or flame. For weeks after hearing that tale Lucy Maud never went out after dark without the fear that she might see this fiery apparition.

A poor ragged old woman, known as Mag Laird, lived in the district. She was harmless, but was the bugbear of children, and especially of Dave. One evening at twilight, when Well, Dave, and Lucy Maud were chasing one another around the hayfield, they suddenly saw, in the direction of the orchard ditch, a strange, shapeless white thing, under a juniper-tree.

"It's *Mag Laird!*" whispered Dave, in terrified accents.

"Nonsense, Dave!" cried Lucy, trying hard to be brave, although her heart was beating madly. "It must be a white calf!"

"It's coming this way!" suddenly screamed Wellington.

It was only too true. The white shape was

creeping down over the ditch in the orchard, as no calf could ever creep! Shrieking, the children started for the house, and tore into Mrs Macneill's bedroom, but alas, she was not there. They then made a stampede for a neighbour's dwelling, where they gasped out their story to grownups who, to their shocked surprise, seemed rather more amused than impressed by it. As they refused to go home, the French-Canadian servants of the household, Peter and Charlotte, were sent out to explore the district. Peter was armed with a pitchfork, and Charlotte carried a pail of oats. They returned very soon to report that no white object could be seen. It had disappeared, evidently. To the children this did not seem strange. Of course a ghost would eventually vanish into thin air.

Presently Grandfather Macneill, having been advised by Peter and Charlotte of the whereabouts of the children, arrived on the scene. When he took them home Grandmother Macneill solved the mystery. She had placed a white tablecloth on the grass under the juniper-tree in the orchard to bleach, and just at dusk, with her knitting in her hand, she went out to retrieve it. She had flung the cloth over her shoulder when her ball of wool fell and rolled over the ditch. Kneeling down, she stretched out her hand in an attempt to grasp it, but the shrieks of the children paralysed her. Before she had time to call out and reassure them they had run away.

This last mundane explanation of the cause of their worst ghost scare had the effect—for a time, at least—of restoring the children to a more down-to-earth attitude.

# VI

## WRECK OF THE "MARCO POLO"

*There's a piping wind from a sunrise shore*
*Blowing over a silver sea,*
*There's a joyous voice in the lapsing tide*
*That calls enticingly;*
*The mist of dawn has taken flight*
*To the dim horizon's bound,*
*And with wide sails set and eager hearts*
*We're off to the fishing ground.*

L. M. MONTGOMERY

ADVENTURES of another kind were always in store for the children. Besides the woods and fields, there was the Cavendish shore, which provided an endless source of entertainment. Part of this shore is rock, where the red cliffs rise steeply from the boulder-strewn coves, and part is a long, gleaming sandy beach which provides a wonderful place for bathing. Then there were the fishing sheds, or houses, as they were called, from which boats went out to catch mackerel. Just at the point where the beach begins stood a little colony of these houses, known as Cawnpore, because news of the Indian Mutiny came at the very moment when the last of the houses was completed. Like many of the other farmers, Lucy Maud's grandfather kept a boat, manned by two or three French-Canadians, for fishing along the shore.

These men often arose at three or four in the morning, and it then became the duty of the children to take them their breakfasts at eight o'clock, and later on their dinner. Sometimes, if the fish 'schooled' all day, they took the men their supper. In this way Lucy Maud came to know every cove, headland, and rock on the shore. During vacations she and the boys would watch the boats through a spy-glass, gather shells, pebbles, and mussels, and sometimes, seated on a rock, devour dulse by the yard. At low tide the rocks were covered with what the children called snails, but which were really periwinkles. Often they found large, empty shells that had been washed ashore from some distant strand or deep-sea haunt. Lucy Maud, who at an early age had memorized Holmes's "The Chambered Nautilus," liked to sit on a large boulder, and, with an empty shell pressed to her ear, recite:

> Build thee more stately mansions, O my soul,
>   As the swift seasons roll;
>   Leave thy low-vaulted past!

*Let each new temple, nobler than the last,*
*Shut thee from Heaven with a dome more vast,*
    *Till thou, at length, art free,*
*Leaving thine outgrown shell by life's unresting*
        *sea.*

In the summer, when she was eight years old, a very exciting event took place. On a stormy, windy day in Cavendish a large sailing-vessel was driven to the beach and wrecked on it. This vessel was none other than the *Marco Polo*, known as the fastest sailing-boat of her class ever built. A strange, romantic history, and many traditions and sailors' yarns, were associated with her. Owing to age, she had been condemned in England under the "Plimsoll Bill," but her owners evaded the Bill by selling her to a Norwegian firm, and then chartering her to bring a cargo of deal plank from Quebec. On her return voyage she was caught in the terrible wind-storm off the Cavendish shore, sprung a leak, and, in a desperate attempt to save cargo and crew, was run ashore by the captain.

Lucy Maud, Well, and Dave were wild with excitement when they heard that a vessel was being driven to the shore. They rushed to the scene, and saw a spectacle they never forgot. Under the threatening sky, and with every stitch of canvas set, a great vessel driven before the

gale was making for the shore. When she was
about three hundred yards from it she grounded,
and the crew immediately cut the rigging, while
the huge masts fell with a crash that could be
heard above the roaring of the storm.

All night the members of the crew stayed on
the doomed ship, but in the morning they came
ashore and sought for lodgings in Cavendish.
There were twenty men of various races—Scottish, Irish, English, Spanish, Norwegian, Dutch,
German, and Tahitian. The two Tahitians, with
their woolly heads, thick lips, and gold earrings,
delighted the children. All were typical tars, and
they soon painted Cavendish a bright red. Their
idea of a good time was to mount a truck-wagon
and go galloping along the roads yelling at the
tops of their voices. They stayed for several
weeks in the settlement, because there was much
business of an official nature to be cleared up in
connexion with the wreck. The captain, a Norwegian, lodged with the Macneills. He was a
well-mannered old fellow, who spoke English
fairly well, although now and then he rather
mixed up his prepositions.

"Thank you for your kindness *against* me,
little Miss Maud," he would say, addressing
Lucy Maud with a grand bow.

As the captain lodged at the Macneill farm,

D

the men of the crew were often on the premises. On the night when they were paid off they sat on the grass under the parlour windows, feeding the old family dog, Gyp, with biscuits. With wondering eyes the children saw the parlour table literally covered with gold sovereigns, which the captain paid to the men. Never in their wildest dreams had they imagined such wealth!

The seashore, and the stories and legends associated with it, saturated Lucy Maud's mind. She listened enthralled to her grandfather's tales of the terrible American gale, or 'Yankee' storm, when hundreds of American fishing-vessels out in the Gulf were wrecked on the north shore. Then there was the story of Cape Leforce, which dated back to the 1760's when the Island of St John (or Ile Saint-Jean) belonged to France. England and France were then at war, and French privateers infested the Gulf, sallying from it to plunder the commerce of the New England colonies. One of these armed vessels, commanded by a captain named Leforce, anchored off the Cavendish shore, and the crew camped for the night on the headland now known as Cape Leforce. The captain and his mate shared a tent, and in endeavouring to divide their booty they quarrelled, and arranged to fight a duel at sunrise. But when the morning came the mate, even while the ground was being marked off for the duel, raised his pistol and shot Captain Leforce dead. He was buried on the spot by his men, and Lucy Maud's grandfather declared that *his* father had seen the grave in his boyhood. The grave long ago crumbled off into the sea, but the name of the unfortunate captain still clings to the red headland.

# VII

## A VISIT TO PARK CORNER

At Park Corner, in a big white house smothered in orchards, lived Lucy Maud's uncle, John Campbell, and one of the great pleasures of her childhood was her annual visit to his hospitable home. Park Corner was thirteen miles from the Macneill farm, and the long drive to it was in itself a joy. The carriage passed along winding roads, by river and shore, with many fascinating glimpses of woods and hills. There were several bridges to cross. Two of them were drawbridges, and of these Lucy Maud was rather frightened. From the moment that the horse stepped on the bridge she felt uneasy, and this feeling persisted until it was safely over the draw. But the spice of supposed danger added to her pleasure, and when she arrived at the big white house she was always sure of a hearty welcome from a trio of merry cousins—Stella, Frederica, and George—who rushed out to drag her in with greetings and laughter.

On one occasion Wellington and Dave accompanied her to Park Corner, and the six children had a marvellous time. The very walls of the hospitable old house seemed to breathe good will and happiness. And there was an old pantry, always stored with cookies, cake, and other tempting edibles, to which the children repaired at bedtime to devour snacks amid much laughter and chatter.

Lucy Maud liked to measure her height by means of an old screw sticking out from the wall on the landing. When she first visited Park Corner as a tiny girl the screw was just on a level with her nose. She now found that her nose rose considerably above it, and from this fact she drew a sense of satisfaction.

The children were very fond of fishing and berry-picking. They fished the brooks up in the woods, using worms for bait. Lucy Maud had some trouble in attaching her squirming worm to the hook, but she managed to catch some fish. One day she caught quite a large trout, and was thrilled with pride, because it was quite as big as those some of the grown-ups had caught. Well and Dave were with her when she caught the trout, and she felt she had gone up five per cent. in their estimation. A girl who could catch a fish like that, they conceded, must be pretty smart.

Berries were to be found in the fields behind the woods, and the children went to them through lanes fragrant with June bells. Sometimes they saw foxes and rabbits in their native haunts. Lucy Maud thought she had never heard anything sweeter than the whistling of the robins at sunset in the maple woods around those fields.

In the kitchen of the Park Corner house stood an old blue wooden chest, on which the children sometimes sat to read or to eat bedtime snacks. This chest was always kept locked, and they loved to speculate about its contents. They were told that it belonged to a certain Eliza Montgomery, a cousin of Lucy Maud's father, and could not be opened until her death. This Eliza Montgomery, now a middle-aged lady, was living in a far-away city. Lucy Maud knew something of her story, and she told the other children a portion of it.

"When Cousin Eliza was as young as Aunt Emily was when she married," she explained, "she fell in love with a very handsome young man, who returned her love. They made up their minds they'd marry, and Cousin Eliza spent a great deal of time in making clothes for the wedding in the spring. She made everything with her own hands, and Grandma says she never saw more lovely handiwork.

"The wedding day arrived. Cousin Eliza was dressed in the beautiful white silk wedding gown she'd made, and she wore a long white bridal veil. Everything was ready for the wedding, but after a while people began to wonder why the bridegroom was so late. What had happened?" Lucy Maud paused dramatically.

"Maybe he'd had an accident," suggested Wellington.

"No, it was worse than that, because the accident wouldn't have been his fault," said Lucy Maud. "It was found he'd run away—all because he was terribly in debt, and was afraid to marry. Poor Cousin Eliza was so broken-hearted that she took all her wedding things and the presents and photograph her lover had given her, and packed them away in this very box we're sitting on. She told Uncle John to keep it for her, and not to open it until after her death."

The pleasant time at Park Corner passed all too quickly. On her return home Lucy Maud experienced a great grief. Cats had always been inhabitants of the Macneill farm. To her grandparents, as well as to herself, a house was not a real home without the "ineffable contentment" of one of these pets, purring before a fire or sitting with tail folded about its feet. A succession of cats owned by the Macneills had died of old age, but there were always specimens of a younger generation on hand. Two charming kittens, by Lucy Maud named Catlin and Pussy Willow, were the latest of these. Lucy Maud was especially fond of Pussy Willow, a very lively kitten, described by her as "the cutest little scrap of grey striped fur" ever seen. One morning soon after her return she found this pet dying of poison, and an agony of grief overwhelmed her as she watched the kitten's bright eyes glazing and her tiny paws growing stiff and cold.

To Lucy Maud the death of the little animal, so innocent and lovable, was an initiation into the mystery of death. In the Eden of her childhood everything had seemed to her everlasting. She had been too young when her mother died to feel deep grief, but now death entered into her world.

In a sense this initiation marked the termination of an epoch in her life. It was not long afterwards that her bright boy companions left the Macneill homestead. In her tenth year Lucy Maud began to take a more realistic view of life.

# VIII

## PRELUDE TO LITERARY LIFE

AMONG the books in the Macneill farm-house were such classics as *The Pilgrim's Progress*, *Pickwick Papers*, *Rob Roy*, *Zanoni*, Hans Andersen's *Fairy Tales*, and the poems of Longfellow, Tennyson, Whittier, Scott, Byron, Milton, and Burns. Lucy Maud pored over the poetry until it became a part of her being. In lines drawn from Whittier or Longfellow, she apostrophized the beauty of flower, hillside and sea, realizing with the poets

> *How fair the realm*
> *Imagination opens to the view.*

Always able to see the funny side of a situation, she had many a laugh over *Pickwick Papers*. The tales of Bulwer Lytton and Scott appealed to the romantic and adventurous side of her nature. And the fairy tales of Hans Andersen were a perpetual delight.

A few magazines came to the house. Grandmother Macneill took *Godey's Lady's Book*. To Lucy Maud this periodical was an unfailing source of entertainment. She enjoyed the fashion plates, showing ladies in high-crowned hats, with bangs and bustles. When she was old enough, she decided, she would wear similar gowns. Godey's magazine contained many romantic short stories and serials, and it seemed to her quite suitable that the heroines should be superlatively beautiful and the villains irremediably wicked.

Only on Sundays was Lucy Maud's choice of reading restricted. The Macneills were good Presbyterians, who thought it wrong to read anything but religious books on the Sabbath. They were regular attendants at the old Presbyterian church, set on a bleak hill, at Cavendish. The family pew was near a window through which the curving rims of the sand hills and beyond them the blue Gulf could be seen, and while her elders prayed Lucy Maud's eyes often wandered to the window.

After church and dinner she was allowed to read either *The Pilgrim's Progress* or Talmage's *Sermons*, and sometimes, as a variation, a thin religious book called *The Memoirs of Anzonetta Peters*. Lucy Maud loved *The Pilgrim's Progress*. Curled up in an old wing-chair, she walked in imagination with Christian and Christiana, and entered into their adventures. She enjoyed also the anecdotes and dramatic word-pictures of the

Talmage *Sermons*. But somehow the biography of Anzonetta Peters seemed nearer to her than the other two books. It was the story of a child who at five years old became converted, grew very ill afterwards, lived a marvellously patient and saintly life for several years, and died, after great sufferings, at the age of ten. Lucy Maud made more than one attempt to imitate this child saint, who never by any chance expressed herself in the ordinary language of childhood, and whose habit it was to respond to any remark addressed to her by a quotation from the Bible or a hymn.

In trying to emulate this holy child, Lucy Maud kept a diary in which she recorded her spiritual progress. On one occasion she wrote, "I wish I were in Heaven now, with Mother, George Whitfield, and Anzonetta B. Peters." The keeping of a diary soon became a daily habit. In it she wrote descriptions of her favourite haunts, biographies of her many cats, histories of visits and school affairs, and critical reviews of books she had read.

When she was ten years old she discovered, on one wonderful day, that she could write poetry. She had been reading Thomson's *Seasons*, and felt inspired to write some blank verses in imitation of him, which she called Autumn. The opening lines were:

Now autumn comes, laden with peach and pear;
The sportsman's horn is heard throughout the
    land;
And the poor partridge, fluttering, falls dead.

The fact that peaches and pears were not abundant, regrettably, in Prince Edward Island, and that the "sportsman's horn" was never heard, did not disturb her. She wrote the precious poem on the back of one of the long red 'letter bills' used in the postal service. Her grandfather kept the local post-office, and three times a week a discarded letter bill came the way of Lucy Maud, who was always short of scribbling-paper.

Just after Lucy Maud had composed this poem, her father from Prince Albert visited the Macneill farm-house, and she proudly showed him the poem.

"Humph!" exclaimed the parent, "it doesn't sound much like poetry to me. Where's the rhyme?"

"It's blank verse," explained his daughter, with dignity.

"Well, it sounds pretty blank to me!" was his disconcerting reply.

But Lucy Maud's poetic impulse was not to be squelched. To please her father, she tried her hand at rhyming, and wrote quantities of verse about flowers, trees, stars, and sunsets. One of

her most ambitious efforts was a long poem
which she called "Evening Dreams," the opening stanza of which was:

> *When the evening sun is setting*
> *Quietly in the west,*
> *In a halo of rainbow glory,*
> *I sit me down to rest.*

She considered this poem her masterpiece. A
lady who was visiting the Macneills at the time
was a rather noted singer. Lucy Maud thought it
would be wonderful if she could get an unbiased
opinion from her of the merits of her poem. She
reasoned that if the lady knew that she, a mere
child, had written it she might not think it worth
while to say what she really thought of it. So she
decided to use strategy.

"Have you ever heard of a song called 'Evening Dreams,' Mrs S——?" she timidly asked her
one evening.

"No, I can't say I have," replied Mrs S——.
"Do you know any of the words of the song?
Perhaps if I heard them I might recognize it."

In a trembling voice Lucy Maud recited the
two opening stanzas, concluding them with a
nervous gasp. But the lady was busy with her
fancy work, and did not appear to notice her
pallor or general shakiness.

"No, I have never heard the song," she commented, "but the words are very pretty."

Lucy Maud was exultant. The opinion of the lady was, she felt, the sweetest morsel of commendation that had yet fallen to her lot. Since she did not know the name of the author, she reasoned, she must have said what she truly meant. The house wasn't big enough to contain her joy. She ran out of it and danced down the lane under the birches in a frenzy of delight, hugging to her heart the remembrance of the singer's words.

In the following winter she made a painstaking copy of "Evening Dreams," using both sides of a sheet of paper, and sent it to the editor of an American magazine called *The Household*. Alas! he proved to be less complimentary than the visitor, and returned the poem promptly, although she had not enclosed a stamp for the purpose. She then sent it to a Canadian publication, with the same results.

Somewhat discouraged, she put her little masterpiece on one side for the time being, and it was not until several years later that she again tried to find a market for her verse.

# IX

## KINDRED SPIRITS

AT twelve years of age Lucy Maud was not the solitary, rather shy, over-sensitive child that she had been in her earlier years. Three years of companionship with two lively boys, given to plain speaking and vigorous living, had served to toughen a too thin skin. She was now able to hold her own with other children, and even to develop qualities of leadership. A born story-teller, she drew around her little groups of girls and boys who were fascinated by her ability to invest everyday scenes and events with a romantic aroma.

Among her schoolmates were two kindred spirits named Amanda and Janie, who agreed that it would be a grand thing to form a Story Club. Having tried her hand at the writing of verse, Lucy Maud thought it would now be in order to experiment with fiction. The three girls each undertook to write a story based on the same plot, which was supplied by Lucy Maud, and to compare the results at a meeting of the Club. The plot was a very tragic one, and had to do with a heroine who was drowned while bathing off the Cavendish beach.

When the girls read their stories aloud at the Story Club meeting Lucy Maud's contribution proved to be by far the most lugubrious of them all. Amanda and Janie agreed that their own tales lacked the depths of misery through which Lucy Maud dragged her heroine. On this basis, they conceded that her story was certainly the best. Encouraged by their attitude, Lucy Maud promptly embarked on the writing of a long story, which she called "My Graves." This story she considered her masterpiece. It dealt with the travels of a Methodist minister's wife, who buried a child in every circuit to which she went with her husband. The oldest was interred in Newfoundland, the youngest in Vancouver, and between these points the countryside was dotted with the graves of her children.

In another story, "The History of Flossy Brighteyes," Lucy Maud related the adventures of a doll. Realizing that she could not kill her waxen beauty, she dragged her through every tribulation short of death. She did let her have a happy old age, however, by allowing her to fall into the hands of a good little girl, who loved her for the dangers through which she had passed, and was very kind to her.

Although in real life Lucy Maud would not have hurt a fly, and wept when a tree had to be cut down or a superfluous kitten drowned, she continued for a time to write stories in which battle, murder, and sudden death were commonplace occurrences. Perhaps the serious nature of the reading she had done at home affected her writing. The spiritual conflicts of Christian in *The Pilgrim's Progress*, and the dangers he encountered, had made a definite impression on her mind. "Life is real, life is earnest," she felt with Longfellow, whose tales of the sorrows of Evangeline and the adventures of Hiawatha she had treasured. And then there was the beloved Anzonetta Peters, the child saint, who died, after great sufferings, at the age of ten.

Actually, Lucy Maud found life so interesting that it never held a dull moment for her. In her vivid imagination she possessed what she called "a passport to Fairyland." By means of it she could at any moment whisk herself into regions of wonderful adventures, unhampered by restrictions of time or place.

"Why don't you use your imagination?" she was fond of saying to some of her friends when they failed to detect anything strange, beautiful, or wonderful in the people or objects she pointed out, such as an old countryman leading a child by

E

the hand, an arch of pale blue sky over trees, a little fern growing in the woods, moonlight falling on a tall birch, or shadow waves rolling over a field of ripe wheat.

In spite of her penchant for tragedy in fiction, her life was full of happy moments. A chum of hers, Alma M——, had also a knack of writing rhyme, and the two girls exercised their common gift in a variety of ways. Birthday greetings, congratulations on some success, notes of sympathy in cases of sickness, were put into rhyme by the young versifiers. They had a habit of getting out together on the old side bench at school, and writing "po'try" on their slates, when the teacher fondly supposed they were sharpening their intellects on fractions.

They began by writing acrostics on their names, and followed this up by addressing poems of fulsome praise to each other. Then they agreed to describe their teachers in stirring verse. The reigning pedagogue was a young man who was noted for his flirtations with Cavendish belles. The two rhymesters wrote some sarcastic effusions dealing with these. They were gleefully comparing their productions when—horrors!— the master himself, who had been standing with his back to them, hearing a class, suddenly wheeled about and took Lucy Maud's slate out of her paralysed hand. She stood up, fully expecting that the end of all things was about to follow, but to her surprise and relief he handed the slate back to her in silence. She sat down with a gasp, and rubbed out the offensive words as speedily as possible, fearing that he might change his mind. She and Alma were so badly scared that they stole no more minutes from school hours in which to write poetry.

# X

## FIRST SUCCESSES

An exciting event occurred when Lucy Maud reached the age of fifteen. Her father sent her a pressing invitation to visit Prince Albert, Saskatchewan, where he hád been living for some years. He had married again, and was anxious to have his daughter meet her stepmother. So one day, under the care of her Grandmother Montgomery, she set forth on her first railway journey. Prince Albert, she discovered, was an excellent place in which to carry on her writing. Her stepmother was a capable housewife, and did not require her services in the domestic sphere. During the day Lucy Maud attended High School.

It was three years since she had sent out "Evening Dreams" to publications which had promptly rejected them. Her ambition to be a poet was now beginning to revive. She thought of the legend her grandfather had told her about old Cape Leforce, and she put it into verse. Then she sent it "down home" to the *Charlottetown Patriot*. Four weeks passed. One afternoon her father came home with a copy of *The Patriot* addressed to her. On opening it she found her verses printed in it, and she tasted all the sweetness of a first literary success. To be sure, she found on reading it carefully that there were some typographical mistakes, which made "the flesh creep on her bones," as she put it, but it was *her* poem, and in a real newspaper!

During the winter she spent in Prince Albert she had other verses and articles printed. A story she had entered in a prize competition was published in the *Montreal Witness*, and a descriptive article on Saskatchewan was not only printed in the *Prince Albert Times*, but copied and commented on favourably by several Winnipeg papers. She sent more poems to the *Charlottetown Patriot*, all of which were published. She began to think that she was somewhat of a literary personage. But hardly had she begun to cherish this rosy view of herself when a rude rebuff restored her to a humbler frame of mind. A story she had sent to the *New York Sun*—on hearing that the paper paid for contributions—came back to her. She descended from her perch, but went on writing. She was beginning to realize the first principle of literary success: "Never give up!"

Summer days, following the year of striving and hard work in Prince Albert, beckoned Lucy

Maud back to her beloved Prince Edward Island.
She spent some months at Park Corner, where
she gave music lessons and wrote more verses
for the *Charlottetown Patriot*. Later on, at the
Cavendish school, she studied for the entrance
examination of the Prince of Wales College.

This College is a publicly owned, non-denom-
inational junior college, which was established at
Charlottetown in 1835. It comprises the last two
years of high school, the first two years of university, a normal school, a school of commerce and
a pre-professional training in medicine, dentistry,
engineering, law and agriculture. It is one of the
best colleges of its kind in the Maritime Provinces and is the Alma Mater of many outstanding Islanders in Canada and abroad, who
cherish and practise its motto: *Ich Dien*.

Proud indeed was Lucy Maud when she
learned that she had passed the entrance examination which would admit her to this fine insti-
tution of higher learning. In the autumn of 1893
she went to Charlottetown to attend the College.
Realizing that every atom of knowledge she
could absorb would contribute to her literary success, she flung herself into her studies. At the
same time she was able to find spare moments
for actual writing.

One day when she called at the post-office she

was handed a thin letter, bearing the address of an American publisher. It proved to be the acceptance of a poem entitled "Only A Violet." The editor offered her two subscriptions to the magazine in payment. Thankfully, she received the subscriptions, one of which she gave to a friend. This was the first tangible reward her pen had brought her.

"It is a start, and I mean to keep on," she wrote in her diary. "Oh, I wonder if I shall ever be able to do anything worth while in the way of writing. It is my dearest ambition."

At Prince of Wales College Lucy Maud studied for a teacher's licence, which she eventually secured. As a teacher, she thought, she would be in a position to carry on her literary work with some success. Her first school was at Bideford, Prince Edward Island. While there she lodged at the Methodist parsonage, of which the mistress was a charming woman who became her great friend. As the minister's wife, this lady not infrequently had to entertain young men of her husband's persuasion. A strange minister came to tea one night, and for the occasion Mrs T—— had made a layer cake, with, as she thought, an especially choice flavouring. With the first bite Lucy Maud realized that there was something wrong, and quickly she put down her piece of cake, keeping her eyes on the minister. To her surprise she saw that he was bravely eating his portion, and that he appeared not to notice the peculiar taste. It was only later that Mrs T—— confided to her the awful truth: by mistake she had flavoured the cake with anodyne liniment. Perhaps the minister, who ate every crumb of his piece of cake, thought he was savouring some new-fangled confection.

While in Bideford, Lucy Maud continued to write in her spare time, but she apparently made little headway. Except in the case of two periodicals that published some of her work without offering her any remuneration, the manuscripts she sent out were returned. At first she used to feel dreadfully hurt when a story or poem over which she had laboured came back with a printed or typed rejection slip. Tears of disappointment *would* come, as she stole away to hide the crumpled manuscript in a drawer, but she remembered her determination never to give up, and she set her teeth and said "I will succeed." She believed in herself, and struggled on alone in secrecy and silence. Deep down, under all discouragements, she had a conviction that one day she would 'arrive.'

# XI

## AT DALHOUSIE COLLEGE

HER first teaching experience did not satisfy the eager mind of Lucy Montgomery. Always anxious to increase and widen her knowledge, her eyes turned to Halifax, where Dalhousie College (as it then was) tried to uphold the principles expounded by its founder, Lord Dalhousie, when he laid the cornerstone in 1820, and declared: "This College of Halifax is founded on the instruction of youth in the higher classics and in all philosophical studies; it is founded in imitation of the University of Edinburgh; its doors open to all who profess the Christian religion."

She decided that she could not do better than to take a course at this College. In the autumn of 1895 she went to Halifax and spent the winter in taking a selected course in English literature at the College. At that time the Professor of English Language and Literature was Archibald MacMechan, who was steadily winning a reputation as an essayist and poet. She quickly fell under the spell of his personality and learning, and she read with avidity all that he had published in prose and poetry.

That winter proved to be well worth while. The contacts she made stimulated her, and she found that she could write with greater facility and effectiveness than before. The year she spent at Halifax was an *annus mirabilis* for her. Not only did she find much intellectual stimulus in her associations at the College, but there came a Big Week during her sojourn in the city when she had three acceptances from editors to whom she had sent stories and poems.

On the Monday of that week she received a letter from the editor of *Golden Days*, a Philadelphia juvenile magazine, accepting a short story she had sent him, and enclosing a cheque for five dollars. On the following Wednesday she received another cheque for five dollars, representing the prize offered by the *Halifax Evening Mail* for the best letter on the theme "Which has the greater patience—man or woman?" Saturday of the same week brought her a cheque for the munificent sum of twelve dollars for a poem she had sent to the *Youth's Companion*, of Philadelphia.

That twenty-two dollars was the first money Lucy Maud's pen had ever earned. She did not squander it in riotous living, nor did she invest it in necessary boots and gloves. She wanted to buy something that would not wear out quickly, and would remind her of that memorable week when she believed that she had at last 'arrived.'

Poetry had been her first love. Now she thought it would be a wonderful thing to have some new and attractive copies of the books of the poets who had helped and inspired her. So one day she went up town and bought five volumes of poetry with the money she had earned by her writing: Tennyson, Byron, Milton, Longfellow, Whittier.

More acceptances followed. Lucy Maud did best with the juvenile stories she sent to Sunday School publications. In her diary she wrote: "I like doing these, but I should like it better if I didn't have to drag a moral into most of them. They won't sell without it, as a rule. So in the moral must go, broad or subtle, as suits the fibre of the particular editor I have in view. The kind of juvenile story I like best to write—and read, too, for the matter of that—is a good, jolly one, 'art for art's sake,' or rather 'fun for fun's sake,' with no insidious moral hidden away in it like a pill in a spoonful of jam!"

"But, oh, I love my work!" she admitted. "I love spinning stories, and I love to sit by the window of my room and shape some 'airy fairy' fancy into verse."

# XII

## STEPPING-STONES TO SUCCESS

AFTER her year at Halifax, Lucy Maud returned to teaching with a renewed self-confidence and a fresh set of values. Naturally fond of children, she taught them with almost missionary zeal, realizing that she was playing at least a small part in the shaping of human destinies. Looking back on her own school days, she remembered how much she had benefited by those intangible influences which flow from the personality of a teacher with high standards. She would give of her best, she resolved. And perhaps among the children she taught there might be potential poets, philosophers, or humanitarians, who later would bear witness to her endeavours in the cause of beauty, kindness, and the pursuit of knowledge.

As for her writing, teaching was in line with that also. The Sunday School papers were buying a good many of her short stories, and some of the children she taught made good 'copy.' At first she tried to write in the evenings, but after a day of strenuous school work she was too tired to concentrate on any form of creative effort. She resolved to rise an hour earlier every morning and devote the time to writing. Her lodging was a very cold farm-house. For five months she arose at six o'clock and dressed by lamplight. At that time no fires were on, but she put on a heavy coat, sat on her feet to keep them from freezing, and, with fingers so cramped that she could scarcely hold her pen, she would write her portion for the day. Sometimes this would be a poem in which she caroled blithely of blue skies, rippling brooks, and June flowers. Then she would thaw out her hands, eat breakfast, and go to school. Those dark, cold winter mornings of her literary apprenticeship severely tested her tenacity and sincerity of purpose.

But a change was coming. In 1898 her Grandfather Macneill died, and her grandmother was left alone in the old homestead. It was unthinkable to Lucy Maud that the woman who had done so much for her since her early childhood should be left in solitude. She resigned her teaching post and returned to Cavendish, where she helped her grandmother with the post-office she kept and gave her spare time to writing. At twenty-four she felt that she could make enough by her pen to keep herself in clothes and to pay for her board. By 1901 she was making what she called a "livable" income for herself. That did not mean that everything she wrote was accepted on its first journey. Nine out of ten manuscripts came back to her, but she sent them out over and over again, and eventually they found resting-places. The story or poem that did not interest one editor, she discovered, sometimes proved to be just what another editor was looking for.

Her method brought results that compensated for delays in publication. On March 21, 1901, she made the following entry in her journal:

"*Munsey's* came today with my poem, 'Comparisons' in it, illustrated. It really *looked* nice. I've been quite in luck of late, for several new and good magazines have opened their portals to this poor wandering sheep of thorny literary ways. I feel that I am improving and developing in regard to my verses. I suppose it would be strange if I did not, considering how hard I study and work. Every now and then I write a poem which serves as a sort of landmark to emphasize my progress. I know, by looking back, that I could not have written it six months, or a year, or four years ago, any more than I could have made a garment the material of which was still unwoven.

"I wrote two poems this week. A year ago, I could not have written them, but now they come easily and naturally. This encourages me to hope

that in the future I may achieve something worth
while. I never expect to be famous. I merely want
to have a recognized place among good workers
in my chosen profession. That, I honestly believe,
is happiness, and the harder to win the sweeter
and more lasting when won."

With such conceptions of the dignity of
writing and teaching, it is small wonder that
Lucy Montgomery made progress. She wrote
modestly that she did not expect to be famous,
but in her steady application to work, motivated
by integrity of purpose, she was laying the
foundation stone for whatever renown might
come to her.

## XIII

## NEWSPAPER WOMAN

LUCY MAUD, after the death of Grandfather Macneill, had promised always to stay with her grandmother, but that did not preclude, of course, occasional visits, or even some short-term work away from home.

In the autumn of 1901 Halifax again beckoned to her. This time she went there to try her hand at newspaper work. There was a vacancy in the office of the *Daily Echo*, the evening edition of the *Halifax Chronicle*, and when Lucy applied for the post she was promptly taken on the staff. At twenty-seven she was a very capable young woman, whose good looks were enhanced by a winning personality.

"I'm a newspaper woman!" she wrote gleefully in her journal of November 11, 1901.

Her duties were various. The *Echo* went to press at two-thirty in the afternoon, but Lucy Maud had to stay in the office until six, to answer the telephone, sign for telegrams, and read proofs. The editing of a page of 'Society letters,' some of which she had to compose herself, and the writing of a weekly column called "Around the Tea-Table," which she signed "Cynthia," comprised the journalistic side of her new post.

"Life in a newspaper office isn't all 'beer and skittles' any more than anything else," she wrote in her journal. "But on the whole it's not a bad life at all. I rather like proof-reading, although it is tedious. The headlines and editorials are my worst thorns in the flesh. Headlines have a natural tendency to depravity, and the editor-in-chief has a ghastly habit of making puns over which I am apt to come to grief. In spite of all my care 'errors will creep in' and then there is the mischief to pay. When I have nightmares now they are of headlines wildly askew and editorials hopelessly hocussed, which an infuriated chief is flourishing in my face."

Lucy Maud's office was a dingy room looking out on a backyard where it seemed to her that all the washerwomen of Halfax assembled. She wrote in her journal:

"The yard is a network of lines from which sundry and divers garments are always streaming gaily to the breezes. On the ground and over the roof cats are prowling continually, and when they fight, the walls resound with their howls. Most of them are lank, starved-looking beasties enough, but there is one lovely gray fellow who

F

basks on a window sill opposite me and looks so much like 'Daffy' that when I look at him, I could squeeze out a homesick tear if I were not afraid that it would wash a clean spot on my grimy face. This office is really the worst place for getting dirty I ever was in."

While performing her rather strenuous duties, the young newspaper woman found that she had little time for her own writing. She was too tired in the evening to attempt creative work. Keeping her clothes in repair and darning her stockings were all she could manage after office hours. She tried to revert to her old habit of getting up at six o'clock in the morning, but she soon realized that the strain of this was too much for her. As a country school-ma'am she had been able to get to bed early, but in the city later hours were in vogue. Then she made an important discovery, about which she wrote in her journal of November 18, 1901:

"Hitherto I had thought that undisturbed solitude was necessary in order that the fires of genius might burn, and even the fire for pot-boiling. I must be alone and the room must be quiet. I could never have even imagined that I could possibly write anything in a newspaper office, with rolls of proof shooting down every

ten minutes, people coming and conversing, tele-
phones ringing, and machines being thumped
and dragged overhead. I would have laughed at
the idea, yea, I would have laughed it to scorn.
But the impossible has happened. I am of one
mind with the Irishman who said you could get
used to anything, even to being hanged!"

Her ability to utilize spare moments under
apparently adverse conditions gave her a new
lease on time. To what good purpose she devoted
this soon became evident in an increasing number of acceptances. In her journal she wrote:

"All my spare time here I write, and not such
bad stuff either, since the *Delineator*, the *Smart
Set*, and *Ainslies'* have taken some of it. I have
grown accustomed to stopping in the middle of
a paragraph to interview a prowling caller, and
to pausing in full career after an elusive rhyme,
to read a lot of proof and snarled-up copy."

Thus, casually, she mentioned some of the
leading American magazines of the day, to which
she began to contribute under such apparently
adverse circumstances. Certainly there was no
danger of her leading an Ivory Tower existence.

The variety of the tasks assigned to her gave
her contacts with all kinds of people. In her
journal of December 9, 1901, she wrote:

"Lately I've been busy with a capital B— 'tending to office work, writing pot-boilers, making Christmas presents, etc., mostly etc. One of the 'etcs.' is a job I heartily detest. It makes my soul cringe. It is bad enough to have your flesh cringe, but when it strikes your soul it gets on your spiritual nerves terribly. We are giving all the firms who advertise with us a free 'write-up' of their holiday goods, and I have to visit all the stores, interview the proprietors, and crystal-lize my information into two 'sticks' of copy. From three to five every afternoon I potter around the business blocks until my nose is purple with the cold and my fingers numb from much scribbling of notes."

But although Lucy Maud's soul might 'cringe' at such assignments, the more earthly part of her nature derived considerable satisfaction from the outcome of at least one of her commercial 'write-ups.' A few days later she wrote in her journal:

"It is an ill wind that blows no good and my disagreeable assignment has blown me some. The other evening I went in to write up 'Bon Marche,' which sets up to be the millinery estab-lishment of Halifax, and I found the proprietor very genial. He said he was delighted that *The*

*Echo* had sent a lady, and by way of encouraging it not to weary in well doing he would send me up one of the new walking hats if I gave the 'Bon Marche' a good write-up. I rather thought he was only joking, but sure enough, when the write-up came out yesterday, up came the hat, and a very pretty one it is too.''

A lively sense of humour sustained Lucy Maud through some of the oddities of her newspaper experience. On December 20, 1901, she wrote:

"The very queerest job up to date came yesterday. The compositors were setting up, for the weekly edition, a serial story called 'A Royal Betrothal,' taken from an English paper, and when about half-way through they lost the copy. Whereupon the news-editor requested me to go to and write an 'end' for the story. At first I did not think I could. What was set up of the story was not enough to give me any insight into the solution of the plot. Moreover, my knowledge of royal love affairs is limited, and I have not yet been accustomed to write with flippant levity of kings and queens. However, I fell to work and somehow got it done. Today it came out, and as yet nobody has guessed where the 'seam' comes in. If the original author ever beholds it, I wonder what he will think.'

Not until the following spring did she learn the reactions of some of *The Echo* readers to *her* ending of "A Royal Betrothal." On May 31, 1901, she made this entry in her journal:

"I had a good internal laugh tonight. I was in a street car and two ladies beside me were discussing the serial that had just ended in *The Echo*. 'You know,' said one, 'it was the strangest story I ever read. It wandered on, chapter after chapter, for weeks, and never seemed to get anywhere; and then it just finished up in eight chapters, *licketty-split*. I can't understand it!' I could have solved the mystery, but I didn't."

On the whole, Lucy Maud undoubtedly derived much benefit from her year of newspaper experience. She learned to make use of material, furnished at first hand or through her imagination, under all kinds of conditions, and so developed her powers of concentration. Newspaper work brought her down to earth, and gave her an insight into human nature on the everyday plane. The necessity of contributing something regularly to a publication—even though it might be of the pot-boiling order which she so much disliked—gave her a facility of expression that later on proved invaluable to her.

# XIV

## A FIRST BOOK ACCEPTED

In June 1902 Lucy Maud returned to her beloved Cavendish, not to leave it again for another nine years. She settled down to writing short stories and serials as before, but at the back of her mind was the thought that she would like to write a book. It had always been her ambition and hope to write one, but she never seemed able to make a beginning. In the case of a short story, when she got the first paragraph written she felt as though it were half done, and the rest came easily, but when she thought of writing a novel the first paragraph became quite a formidable undertaking.

The thought persisted, however. In the spring of 1904 she was looking over a notebook, in which she jotted down ideas for plots, incidents, characters, and descriptions, when she ran across a faded entry written many years before: "Elderly couple apply to orphan asylum for a boy. By a mistake a girl is sent them." She thought this might do as the theme of a short serial she wanted to write for a Sunday School paper, and she began to block out the chapters, devise and select incidents, and "brood up" her heroine.

She brooded to such good effect that the character of Anne emerged, and began to take form in such a fashion that she soon seemed very real to her creator. and took possession of her to an unusual extent. Anne appealed to her so strongly that she began to think it would be rather a shame to waste her on an ephemeral little serial, and the thought came again, "Write a book."

The central idea, she felt, was there, and all she had to do was to spread it out over enough chapters to make a volume.

And so Lucy Maud began her first novel. She wrote it in the evenings after her regular day's work was done. Seated at the window of the little gable room of the farm-house, which for so many years had been hers, she started the book in the spring of 1904 and finished it in the October of 1905. She typed the manuscript herself, using an old, second-hand machine that, in her own words, "never made the capitals plain and wouldn't print 'w' at all."

Thinking that it might stand a better chance of acceptance with a new rather than an old publisher, she submitted it to an American firm that had recently come to the front with several best sellers. But the new firm very promptly sent it back to her.

Then she tried one of the old, established firms but that, too, returned it. Next she thought it might be a good idea to try firms that were neither old nor new. Four of these returned the manuscript with a cold, printed note of rejection but one of them wrote, "Our readers report that they find some merit in your story, but not enough to warrant its acceptance."

This "damning with faint praise" was more than Lucy Maud could stand. She put her *Anne* away in an old hat-box in the clothes room, intending one day to reduce her to the original seven chapters she had planned for a serial, which might bring her thirty-five or even forty dollars. The manuscript lay in the hat-box until the author ran across it one winter day while rummaging. She turned over the pages, reading bits here and there. Somehow it did not seem to her to be so very bad.

"I'll try once more," she resolved.

Off the manuscript went again, and this time it did not speedily return. Lucy Maud's hopes began to grow when after a month's absence she was still left in the dark as to its fate. Six weeks passed, and still no word came. Then on one memorable day a letter arrived from the American publisher to whom she had sent her resurrected Anne. With trembling fingers she tore it open, and then gave a whoop of joy. Her manuscript had been accepted!

The enterprising firm that accepted the first book of an unknown writer was L. C. Page and Company, of Boston. It is said that an intelligent stenographer on the office staff of the firm, who was sometimes employed as a reader, was so much impressed by the merits of the manuscript that she urged her employers to publish it. Deciding to take a chance on it, the Boston firm bought Anne outright for five hundred dollars, an amount which seemed large to the author at the time.

That night Lucy Maud wrote in her journal:

"Well, I've written my book! The dream dreamed years ago at that old brown desk in school has come true at last after years of toil and struggle. And the realization is sweet, almost as sweet as the dream. . . . The book may or may not succeed. I wrote it for love, not money, but very often such books are the most successful, just as everything in the world that is born of true love has life in it, as nothing constructed for mercenary ends can ever have."

# XV

# FAME

ALTHOUGH her book had at last been accepted, Lucy Maud had to wait another year before it was actually published. Then, on June 20, 1908, she wrote in her journal:

"Today has been, as *Anne* herself would say, 'an epoch' in my life. My book came today 'spleet-new' from the publishers. I candidly confess that it was to me a proud and wonderful and thrilling moment. There, in my hand, lay the material realization of all the dreams and hopes and ambitions and struggles of my whole conscious existence—my first book. Not a great book, but mine, mine, mine, something which I had created."

Little did she anticipate the reception which her first book received! Always modest, she had envisaged "a very moderate success indeed"—if the book succeeded at all. She never dreamed that it would appeal to young and old. She thought that girls in their teens might like to read it, and they comprised the only audience she hoped to reach.

How different was the reality! Success came not gradually but immediately. Hundreds of letters from all over the world poured into the home of the modest, thirty-four-year-old author, not only from children, but from soldiers in India, missionaries in China, traders in Africa, monks in far-away monasteries, and from trappers in the Canadian North. Grey-haired men and women, Supreme Court justices and heads of households, were moved to laughter or tears by quaint sayings and doings of Anne, the child who expressed herself in a rather pedantic fashion, and yet had such a convincing and unalloyed naturalness of behaviour.

Little girls who could think of Anne in no other way than as a real living entity wrote touching letters addressed to "Miss Anne Shirley, Green Gables, Avonlea, Prince Edward Island." One child, who had been much taken by the character of Matthew in *Anne of Green Gables*, began her letter with, "My dear long-lost uncle," and claimed that he was her Uncle Lionel, who had disappeared years ago.

Several people wrote to her that their lives would make very interesting stories, and generously offered to give her 'half the proceeds' in return for 'the facts.' Lucy Maud answered only one of these letters, that from a young man who had enclosed stamps for a reply. She told him, as kindly as possible, that she already had sufficient material for books that it would take her ten years to write. Undaunted, he wrote back that he had "a great deal of patience," and would cheerfully wait until ten years had expired, and then he would write again.

The sale of the book was helped by the comments of outstanding critics and writers. "Anne,' declared Bliss Carman in a review, "is one of the immortal children of fiction." Mark Twain pronounced her to be "the sweetest creation of child life yet written."

Among her numerous correspondents were those who made inquiries of the author about the originals of the scenes and characters described in her books. Lucy Montgomery, without doubt, drew largely on her own experiences in all her work, but it should be remembered that to her the world of imagination was almost as real as that of concrete fact, and in drawing upon the events of her past life she often recorded episodes that belonged as much to this realm as to her ordinary, everyday life.

*Is Cavendish Avonlea?* This was a question she was frequently asked, and she replied:

"Cavendish is 'Avonlea' to a certain extent. "Lover's Lane' is a very beautiful lane through the woods on a neighbour's farm. It was a beloved haunt of mine from my earliest days. The 'Shore Road' has a real existence, between Cavendish and Rustico. But the 'White Way of Delight,' 'Wiltonmere,' and 'Violet Vale' were transplanted from the estates of my castles in Spain."

*Is the Lake of Shining Waters Cavendish Pond?* was another popular inquiry. To this she replied:

"The pond I had in mind is the one at Park Corner, below Uncle John Campbell's house. But I suppose that a good many of the effects of light and shadow I had seen on the Cavendish Pond figured unconsciously in my descriptions. Anne's habit of naming places was an old one of my own. I named all the pretty nooks and corners about the old farm. I had, I remember, a 'Fairyland,' a 'Dreamland,' a 'Pussy-Willow Palace,' a 'No Man's Land,' a 'Queen's Bower,' and many others. The 'Dryad's Bubble' was purely imaginary, but the 'Old Log Bridge' was a real thing. It was formed by a single large tree that had blown down and lay across the brook. It had served as a bridge to the generation before my time, and was hollowed out like a shell by the

tread of hundreds of passing feet. Earth had
grown into the crevices, and ferns and grasses
had found foot and fringed it luxuriantly. Velvet
moss covered its sides and below was a deep,
clear, sun-flecked stream.''

*Are David and Margaret Macneill the prototypes
of Anne's foster-parents, Matthew and Marilla
Cuthbert?*

"In a sense," Lucy Maud replied. She did
admit, however, that the entry in her notebook
which led to Anne of Green Gables—"Elderly
couple apply to orphan asylum for a boy; a girl
is sent them," had been suggested by the arrival
of a niece at the home of David and Margaret
Macneill, a bachelor and his sister, who lived at
Cavendish, and her own conjectures about her.
She wondered whether the child was an orphan,
and what the outcome would be if the brother
and sister had wanted a boy and had been sent
instead a girl. But the niece, who was not an
orphan, was not the prototype of Anne. Nor were
her uncle and aunt the exact prototypes of
Matthew and Marilla Cuthbert.

On the subject of 'originals' of her characters,
Lucy Maud expressed herself very clearly.

"Ever since my first book was published," she
wrote, "I have been persecuted by the question,

'Was so-and-so the original of such-and-such in your book?' And behind my back they don't put it in the interrogative form, but in the affirmative. I know many people who have asserted that they are well acquainted with the 'originals' of my characters. Now, for my own part, I have never . . . met one human being who could, as a whole, be put into a book without injuring it. Any artist knows that to paint *exactly* from life is to give a false impression of the subject. *Study* from life, he must, copying suitable heads or arms, appropriating bits of character, personal or mental idiosyncrasies, 'making use of the real to perfect the ideal.' But the ideal, his ideal, must be behind and beyond it all. The writer must *create* his characters, or they will not be life-like."

*Is Green Gables your own home?* was another question L. M. Montgomery was frequently asked.

"No," she always emphatically replied. But as even to-day misconceptions exist on this subject, a few explanatory words may not be amiss. The house now called Green Gables, in Cavendish National Park, was originally a farmstead belonging to David and Margaret Macneill. L. M. Montgomery's childhood and youth were spent in the farm home of her grandparents, who were also Macneills. For this reason, when Green

Gables is referred to as the "old Macneill farm,"
it is sometimes assumed that the author used her
own old home as a domicile for Anne. As a
matter of fact, L. M. Montgomery's old home—
also a Macneill farm—was pulled down some
years ago, and now nothing of it remains but the
cellar.

Some years later the vexed question of copy-
right came up to trouble her peaceful existence.
The Boston company which had bought her first
book outright for 500 dollars had complete control of it and all rights pertaining to it. But they
had not the right to publish any of her other
work without her permission, so when in 1920
this company brought out some of her longer
short stories in a book, and failed to consult her
about the matter, she sued them for unauthorized
publication, and a case began before the courts
which was to last for nine years before it brought
her ultimate victory.

In 1921 she was subjected to another trial.
This occurred when she saw Hollywood's silent
version of *Anne of Green Gables*, starring Mary
Miles Minter. She was obliged to witness, with
ill-concealed indignation, a rendering of Anne of
which she did not approve. Mary Miles Minter,
she contended, was "too sugary sweet—not a
scrap like gingery Anne." Then, too, she was

G

affronted by the transferring of the scene of Green Gables to the United States, and she saw with angry eyes the Stars and Stripes flying over Anne's school! As she had sold her book outright to this company, she had received nothing for the film rights, and had no control over the treatment of the story.

## XVI

## LAST YEARS AT CAVENDISH

FAME had come to Lucy Maud Montgomery in her quiet home at Cavendish, and soon it looked as if another of the coveted joys of humanity might be hers. She was often seen in the company of a certain tall and good-looking clergyman, who was pastor of a small Presbyterian church not far from Cavendish. True, she and the young man had been good friends for a number of years, but her relatives had an idea that now she had realized her ambition and published a book she would settle down to matrimony.

The minister was the Rev. Ewan Macdonald, whose great-grandfather—a member of the clan known as Macdonald of the Isles and of Sleat— had come out to Canada at the age of seven from the Island of Skye in the Hebrides.

Born at Valleyfield, Prince Edward Island, in 1870, Ewan Macdonald had attended Prince of Wales College at Charlottetown, and had then gone to Dalhousie College and Pine Hill Seminary. With similar tastes and background, the two young people had been almost immediately attracted to each other when they first met in 1901. If the minister had been allowed to follow the dictates of his heart Lucy Maud would have become very shortly his bride. She had promised her grandmother, however, that as long as she lived she would not leave her, and she held steadfastly to her word.

Then began for Ewan Macdonald years of waiting for the woman he loved. He gave up several opportunities of securing larger and more lucrative ministerial posts, in order to remain near her. When Lucy Maud's *Anne of Green Gables* was published in 1908 he hoped that she would associate his seven years of waiting for her with the seven that Jacob had served when he waited for Rachel, but Lucy Maud's grandmother still lived, and she held steadily to her promise not to leave her.

Besides that, her brain was teeming with stories demanding to be made into books without delay. In 1909 *Anne of Avonlea* came out, and it was followed in 1910 by *Kilmeny of the Orchard*. This latter story had really been written several years before *Anne of Green Gables*, and under another name had appeared in serial form in a magazine, so she was rather amused when several perspicacious reviewers commented that the Kilmeny book showed "the insidious influence of popularity and success" in its style and plot.

During 1910 she wrote a book which she confessed gave her the greatest pleasure to write of all her books. This was *The Story Girl*, and as she worked at it she felt that its characters and landscapes were very real to her.

In this collection of thirty-two stories, Lucy Montgomery drew largely for subject matter on tales told to her by her grandparents and by her Great-aunt Lawson, whose fund of story material seemed inexhaustible. The story entitled "How Betty Sherman Won a Husband" obviously is founded on a fire-side tale told her by her Grandfather Macneill. He had related that her great-grandmother, Betsey Penman, had actually proposed to her great-grandfather, David Montgomery. (See Chapter I.) Or take the story "The Blue Chest of Rachel Ward," and we can trace the original of this in the tale about the old blue chest that stood in the kitchen of John Campbell's house at Park Corner. (See Chapter 6.) Lucy Maud admitted that this particular story was almost literally true.

"All the children in the book are purely imaginary," L. M. Montgomery explained, in answer to inquiries. "The old 'King Orchard' was a compound of our orchard in Cavendish and the orchard at Park Corner. 'Peg Bowen' was suggested by a half-witted, gypsy-like personage who roamed at large for many years over the Island and was the terror of my childhood. We children were always being threatened that if we were not good Peg would catch us. The threat did not make us good, it only made us miserable.

"Poor Peg was really very harmless, when she was not teased or annoyed. If she were, she could be vicious and revengeful enough. In winter she lived in a little hut in the woods, but as soon as the spring came the lure of the open road proved too much for her, and she started on a tramp which lasted until the return of the winter snows. She was known over most of the Island. She went bareheaded and barefooted, smoked a pipe, and told extraordinary tales of her adventures in various places. Occasionally she would come to church, stalking unconcernedly up the aisle to a prominent seat. She never put on hat or shoes on such occasions, but when she wanted to be especially grand she powdered face, arms and legs with *flour*!"

*The Story Girl* was the last piece of fiction that was written in her old home by the gable window where she had spent so many happy hours of creation.

Changes of a vital nature were impending, but only the future could reveal their course. Meanwhile her life with her Grandmother Macneill continued its peaceful tenor.

# XVII

## MARRIAGE AND HONEYMOON

EVER since her grandfather's death in 1898, except for the year she had spent at Halifax as a newspaper woman and some brief visits to Park Corner, Lucy Maud had remained at home with her Grandmother Macneill. In the early part of 1911 it became evident that the woman who had for so many years taken the place of a mother in her life had not much longer to live, and it was not a surprise to her devoted granddaughter when in the winter of 1911, at the age of eighty-seven, she died. With her passing the old homestead was broken up. Lucy Maud could not bear to remain there alone, and she was glad to move to her Uncle John Campbell's house at Park Corner, where she was always a welcome guest. It was from this house that, in the following July, she was quietly married to the man who had waited patiently for her through the years.

Although she was thirty-six years of age when she married the Rev. Ewan Macdonald, she looked much younger. He was five years older, and in his sight Lucy was still the young girl he had loved when he went into the Cavendish post-office to buy stamps, as far back as 1901—the pretty girl with the almost jet-black hair and deep blue eyes. Neither the years nor fame had spoiled her. Her face reflected an inner tranquillity, won by her adherence to spiritual evaluations. "It has always seemed to me, ever since early childhood," she once wrote, "that amid all the commonplaces of life I was very near to a kingdom of ideal beauty. Between it and me hung only a thin veil. I could never draw it quite aside, but sometimes a wind fluttered it and I caught a glimpse of the enchanting realm beyond—only a glimpse—but those glimpses have always made life worth while."

On her wedding trip to England and Scotland another dream of her youth came true. As usual, she kept a diary, and it is interesting to read some of her impressions, viewed through the lens of her personality. Of her trip to Iona she wrote:

"It was a typical Scottish day, bright and sunny one hour, showery or misty the next. . . . The wild scenery of cape and bay, island and bleak mountain—the whole of course peppered with ruined ivy castles—was an ever-changing panorama of interest peopled with the shades of

the past. . . . Iona is interesting as the scene of
St Columba's ministry. His ancient cathedral is
still there. Of greater interest to me was the
burial place of the earliest Scottish kings, about
sixty of them, it is said, finishing with that Duncan who was murdered by Macbeth. They were
buried very simply, those warriors of ancient
days. There they lie, in their island cemetery,
beneath the gray sky. Neither 'storied urn nor
animated bust' mark their resting place. Each
grave is covered simply by a slab or worn, carved
stone. . . . I would have liked to have spent several
days in Iona, prowling by myself around its
haunted ruins and getting acquainted with its
inhabitants."

At the Burns monument the interesting feat-
ure to her was a lock of Highland Mary's fair
hair and the Bible upon which she and Burns
swore their troth in their parting tryst.

"Poor sweet Highland Mary!" she wrote in
her journal. "I don't suppose she was anything
more than a winsome little country lass, no
sweeter or prettier than thousands of other
maidens who have lived and died, if not unwept,
at least unhonoured and unsung. But a great
genius flung over her the halo of his love and
lo! she is one of the immortals."

On their way to Inverness, the Macdonalds stopped at Kirriemuir (Barrie's "Thrums").

"One thing about it made me feel at home—its paths, which Barrie calls 'pink,' are the very red of our own island roads. I could have fancied that I was prowling in the woods around Lovers' Lane."

Portions of Scotland were "so like Cavendish" that they made her feel bitterly homesick. In describing a visit to Norham Castle, she wrote:

"Growing all over the grounds was a little blue flower which I never saw anywhere else save in the front orchard of my old home in Cavendish. Grandmother Woolner had brought it out from England with her. It gave me an odd feeling of pain and pleasure mingled, to find it growing there around that old ruined Scottish castle which seemed to belong so utterly to another order of things."

While in York she discovered something for which she had long searched. One of her cherished memories was of a pair of china dogs which she had seen as a child on a visit to her Grandfather Montgomery. They were white with green spots all over them, and her father had told her that whenever they heard the clock strike twelve at midnight they bounded down on to the hearth and barked. Those dogs had been purchased in England, and she thought it not unlikely that there she might discover a similar pair. Her journal entry says:

"Yesterday in a little antique shop near the great Minster I found a pair of lovely dogs and snapped them up on the spot. To be sure they have no green spots. The race of dogs with green spots seems to have become extinct. But my pair have gold spots and are much larger than the old Park Corner dogs. They are over a hundred years old and I hope they will preside over my Lares and Penates with due dignity and aplomb."

In September, replete with sight-seeing, they sailed for home. The Rev. Ewan Macdonald had accepted a call to the Presbyterian church at Leaskdale, Ontario, and it was in the manse of this small Ontario community, not very far from Toronto, that Lucy Maud Montgomery took up the serious task of being a minister's wife.

The Rev. Ewan Macdonald brought home as his bride a famous woman, and the return of the newly wedded couple was heralded by the newspapers of Prince Edward Island and Ontario. At Toronto the local branch of the Canadian Women's Press Club (founded in 1904) held a

reception at the King Edward Hotel in honour
not only of Mrs Ewan Macdonald, but of another
bride, Mrs Donald MacGregor, known to the
literary world by her pen name of Marian Keith.
At the time of the meeting of the two brides
Mrs MacGregor, like Mrs Macdonald, had written four books—*Duncan Polite*, published in
1905, *The Silver Maple*, *Treasure Valley*, and
*'Lizbeth of the Dale*. Between the two authors an
instinctive liking developed which ripened into a
real friendship that lasted through the years.

It was a chilly evening in late September when
the travel-weary bride and groom entered the
Manse at Leaskdale. She had loved the old Macneill homestead, but, after all, it had belonged
not to her own father and mother but to her
grandparents. Now she felt the real pride of
ownership. A fire burned on the hearth, and from
the rug before it arose with stately dignity a
large grey cat. This was Queenie, the first of the
many domestic pets that always formed a part of
the family life of the Macdonalds. There was the
mantel on which she would place the china dogs
brought from England; there were home-made
rugs on the floor, comfortable chairs; and—
above all—books scattered everywhere. "What
more could we want?"

Although she was now a minister's wife, Lucy

Maud realized that writing must be given a certain priority in her life, and her husband recognized this also. No Victorian male, he was proud of his gifted wife. With the money earned from her writing she was able to secure the services of competent household assistants. This enabled her to set aside certain hours every day for creative work. In the year that followed her coming to Leaskdale two books by her were published: *Chronicles of Avonlea* and *Rilla of Ingleside*, and her pen was already at work on other novels.

# XVIII

## WIFE AND MOTHER

"At the Manse, Leaskdale, Ont., on Sunday, July 7th, 1912, to Rev. E. and Mrs Macdonald, a son." So ran the newspaper announcement of a very important event. She who had experienced the thrills of successful authorship when her novel came "spleet-new" from the publishers, now knew a greater joy when her baby, "spleet-new," was placed in her arms.

A friend had given her a Baby's Book, and in it are recorded the details of Chester Cameron's babyhood, early childhood and youth up to his seventeenth year—a rather prolonged period of juvenescence. Three years after the birth of Chester, on October 7, 1915, a second son was born to the Macdonalds. This was Stuart, who soon advanced from the toddler stage to companionship with his big brother.

Now her time was indeed well taken up, with two lively boys, her writing, household and church duties, and talks before various clubs. She was a member of the Canadian Women's Press Club of Toronto and of the Hypatia Club of

Uxbridge, and was often called upon to contribute papers on various themes, or to attend and address scattered literary and church groups throughout Ontario.

On the subject of women Lucy Montgomery had decided opinions. Her son Chester quotes her as saying, "I have no desire to be equal to man. I prefer to maintain my superiority." Like Virginia Woolf, she believed that women had a contribution to make to society peculiarly their own, and she deplored a tendency on the part of some feminists to adjudge feminine progress by masculine standards. In her paper on "Womanhood in Browning," she stressed the intuitive and spiritual qualities of women, their faith and imagination, which so often came to the aid of men in time of need, providing for them "islands of meaning" in a disordered world.

The supernatural in modern fiction was another subject that appealed to her. In several of her stories—and especially in the Emily books which are largely autobiographical in content—she relates experiences that have to do with telepathy, second sight, and ghostly apparitions.

Among the members of the Hypatia Club who were particular friends of hers were Mrs H. Leask, Mrs J. A. McClintock, Mrs Mark Weldon, and Mrs R. F. Willis, all of whom appre-

L. M. MONTGOMERY MACDONALD IN 1917

THE REV. EWAN MACDONALD WITH CHESTER (*right*)
AND STUART (*left*)

ciated her literary talents. They did find her just a little "aloof," and the fact that she usually wore "two veils" at the meetings amused them, but in her contributions to the Club they admired her wit and humour as well as her philosophical concepts.

Between 1914 and 1926 were written *The Golden Road, Anne of the Island, Anne's House of Dreams, Rainbow Valley, Emily of the New Moon, Emily Climbs,* and *The Blue Castle.* She had a large fan mail, and tried to keep in touch with all her correspondents. To personal friends she sometimes wrote letters that were twenty or thirty pages long. She possessed a camera which she could operate with professional skill. To her friend, Marian Keith, she sent a charming picture of herself in a daisy field, on the back of which she had written:

> *Gather daisies while you may,*
> *Time brings only sorrow,*
> *And the daisies of today*
> *Will just be weeds tomorrow.*

(a long way) *after* HERRICK

In 1916 a collection of poems was brought out by her under the title of *The Watchman and other Poems.* The book was published by Frederick A. Stokes of New York, and dedicated "To the memory of the gallant Canadian soldiers who

H

have laid down their lives for their country and their empire." The poems reveal some of the qualities that make her novels popular—a joy in being alive and responsive to the beauty of nature and the kindredship of souls. Most of them have to do with memories of her youth and life in Prince Edward Island. "The Watchman" is a religious narrative poem in blank verse. With dramatic force the author contrasts the fury and violence of those responsible for the Crucifixion with the tremendous love that conquered them, and her hero exclaims, after the impact of that love:

> *I care no more for glory; all desire*
> *For conquest and for strife is gone from me,*
> *All eagerness for war; I only care*
> *To help and heal bruised beings, and to give*
>   *Some comfort to the weak and suffering.*

The Macdonalds were happy in their home life, although sorrow had visited them in 1914, when an infant boy, born on August 13, lived only one day. He was baptized Hugh and a tiny grave was made for him in the Foster Memorial Cemetery, which lies midway between Leaskdale and Uxbridge. To his mother his existence was very real. She always thought of him as a third son.

The long summer vacations were usually spent

by the family in trips to Muskoka or Prince Edward Island. A horse and buggy had been their means of transportation for a time, but when their good grey mare died—of course, of old age—they invested in a car, which they named Lady Jane Grey. She was put to much use in trips to Uxbridge, Aurora, Toronto, and other surrounding parts. The boys delighted in her, and Chester soon learned to drive her. Much use made Lady Jane Grey a little unstable, and she became subject to breakdowns. Sometimes the Macdonalds found themselves stranded in out-of-the-way places where it was difficult to get repairs quickly done.

But in spite of these disadvantages the family decided in 1925 to make a trip to Prince Edward Island in their car. To be out of doors and together for hours at a time, with the canopy of the stars above them at night when they slept on their camp mattresses, and with beds and meals in remote wayside inns when it rained, compensated them for inconveniences. At length, after many delays, due to weather conditions or the need for repairs to Lady Jane Grey, they arrived at their destination.

When once Lucy Maud set foot on the red soil of her beloved island she forgot all her troubles.

"Peace!" she wrote to her friends. "You never know what peace is until you walk on the shores or in the fields or along the winding red roads of Prince Edward Island in a summer twilight when the dew is falling and the old stars are peeping out and the sea keeps its mighty tryst with the little land it loves. You find your soul then. You realize that youth is not a vanished thing, but something that dwells forever in the heart."

She loved to visit relatives and friends, and to talk over old times with them. One of her former schoolmates was Mrs R. E. Mutch, who still lives at Charlottetown. Fanny Wise, as she was then, and Lucy Maud had sat together when they attended Prince of Wales College, away back in 1893. They were great friends, and liked to reminisce.

"Do you remember how I used to send you my cheques to put in the bank when I was teaching school in Bideford, Fanny—after I left College?" Lucy Maud inquired.

"Indeed I do! And I remember how impressed I was by one of the cheques for three hundred dollars that you received for a story in the *Ladies' Home Journal*."

Lucy Maud laughed. "Ah, that was certainly an epoch in my life at that time, as Anne would say! More often than not, I received only five dollars, or at most ten."

"You put up your hair when you started teaching, Maud," Mrs Mutch reminded her, "but at College do you remember how you used to have it long and flowing below your knees?"

"Well, I was rather proud of my hair," explained Lucy Maud, "but I certainly must have looked a little odd."

"And I remember you always wore three little pink bows in your dresses," her friend reminisced. "Yes, you did look rather out of the common; but then, as you say in one of your stories, 'It's the peculiar folks who give colour to life.'"

Among other old friends Lucy Maud enjoyed visiting were Mr and Mrs Harlan Found. The Founds live at Charlottetown, but own a summer cottage at Clifton, none other than the small house in which Lucy Maud was born in 1874. Of course, she took her husband and sons on a pilgrimage to this place, which the owners had transformed into a very attractive summer abode.

Another beloved spot she delighted in visiting was the old Campbell house at Park Corner— the comfortable, hospitable farmstead in which she had passed so many happy and unforgettable days and nights. The trio of merry cousins with whom she had played as a child—Stella, Frederica, and George—were now all married. The girls were, respectively, Mrs McKellar and Mrs McFarlane. George had married Ella Montgomery, whose mother, Elizabeth Montgomery, was a cousin of Lucy Maud's father.

This interesting old house was owned first by the late James Townsend Campbell, J.P., who was known as "Squire Campbell." He was married twice, first to a daughter of Donald Montgomery, M.P., and, after her death, to Elizabeth Montgomery, sister of the late Senator Montgomery. When Lucy Maud, as a little girl, went on visits to Park Corner the owner of the old house was John Campbell, who was a son of "Squire" Campbell. He was succeeded by his son George—one of Lucy Maud's old playmates—whose son, James Townsend Campbell, is now in possession of the old homestead.

# XIX

## THE EMILY BOOKS

Not long after the return of the Macdonalds from their trip to Prince Edward Island in 1925 the Rev. Ewan Macdonald received a call to Norval, Ontario. With great regret his Leaskdale congregation, after his long years of faithful service, parted with him. The truth was that he was not in very good health. At Norval his pastoral duties made less tax on his energies, and he was able to fulfil them with his usual fidelity.

L. M. Montgomery now had fourteen books to her credit. At Norval she completed her "Emily" trilogy with *Emily's Quest*. This is a notable trilogy, and it deserves to take a high place in Canadian literature. All the characteristics of the author—her humour, insight into human nature, and love of nature and animals—are evidenced in it. Although it is commonly supposed that the Anne books are more autobiographical than her other novels, it should be remembered that from an early age writing was the predominant interest in Lucy Maud's life, and this fact is emphasized, not in the Anne books, but in the Emily trilogy. Of course, there was a good deal of Anne in Lucy Maud, but there is also much of Anne in Emily. The point is that Emily is a more complete reflection of Lucy Maud Montgomery than is Anne.

Even in the minor matter of personal appearance, the picture drawn of Emily is more in accord with Lucy Maud's own appearance than are the red hair and freckles of Anne. Yet to support his theory, elaborated at some length, that L. M. Montgomery was in reality Anne, the writer of a 'flashback' in *Maclean's* magazine claims that Lucy Maud's looks resembled those of Anne, and that her hair, if not actually red, was "reddish." The fact is that Lucy Maud's hair in youth was—like Emily's—almost jet-black.

"I'd say that the Emily books are altogether more autobiographical than the Anne ones," declared her son, Chester Cameron Macdonald, in referring to the matter. "As for her hair, until it turned gray, it was certainly black."

Pages from *Emily of the New Moon* read like pages from Lucy Maud's own life. Emily, like her, was a solitary child, dependent on relatives when her parents died for her upkeep. She too was consoled by imaginary companions with whom she conversed and by her love of animals and reading. She made friends with the trees and brooks, just as Lucy Maud did, and gave them names. Emily's taste in books corresponded with that of Lucy Maud. She loved *The Pilgrim's Progress*, Thomson's *Seasons*, *Alice in Wonderland*, and *The Memoirs of Anzonetta B. Peters*, the child saint, who was converted at five and died at ten. Like Lucy Maud again, Emily began to write poetry when she was ten years old, and the first poem she produced was called—like Lucy Maud's first poem—"Autumn," and had the same opening lines. She wrote it, just as the other child had done, on a 'letter-bill,' obtained from the post-office kept by her relatives.

Emily's school-days and experiences are almost identically the same as those of Lucy Maud. Both children suffered the penalty of being 'different' from the ordinary run of childhood, and aroused the antagonism of their school mates.

"Why don't you like me?" Emily asked one of her attackers.

"Because you ain't a bit like us," was the prompt reply.

Emily, like Lucy Maud, was obliged to wear "buttoned boots" to school, when all the other girls went barefooted. She also had to wear the "baby aprons" which caused poor Lucy Maud so much humiliation. Eventually, however, Emily, like Lucy Maud, won a place for herself at school.

She was accepted by her companions as a girl of spirit, who could give and take with the best of them. Sometimes she and the "kindred spirits" she was always discovering got into mischief by writing "po-try" in school hours, or by mimicking the peculiarities of the current teacher.

Emily's "supreme moment" came when she received, like Lucy Maud, a "thin letter," with the address of a publishing firm on it—"*promisingly thin*, so different from the *plump letters* full of rejected verses" which she was accustomed to receive. The "thin letter" contained her first acceptance, and she was offered as a reward two subscriptions to the magazine in which her verses were to appear. Almost step by step, Emily's mounting of the ladder of literary success corresponded with Lucy Maud's climb, right to the point where she recorded in her diary the wonderful news that her first book had been accepted by an American publisher.

From a perusal of the three Emily books the youthful literary aspirant may obtain many stimulating and useful suggestions or pointers, as applicable to-day as when Emily wrote. Like other writers who have achieved success, Emily realized at an early age that she wanted to be an author. When she was twelve years old a friend sent her "The Fringed Gentian," a poem which greatly influenced her resolve to keep on writing until she reached the goal she had set for herself. Here are some of the lines from it:

> *Then whisper, blossom, in thy sleep*
> *How I may upward climb*
> *The Alpine Path, so hard, so steep,*
> *That leads to heights sublime.*
> *How I may reach that far-off goal*
> *Of true and honoured fame*
> *And write upon its shining scroll*
> *A woman's humble name.*

When she read these lines, it is related, Emily took a sheet of paper and wrote on it:

I, Emily Byrd Starr, do solemnly vow this day that I will climb the Alpine Path and write my name on the scroll of fame.

Lucy Maud was also much impressed by "The Fringed Gentian," and after reading it she made a similar vow.

Having formulated her objective, Emily worked with steady persistence toward achieving it. Like Lucy Maud, she read widely and studied hard. She took courses in English literature, and listened with keen interest to the advice of those she realized could help her. By reading and writing poetry, and by communion with nature, she cultivated her imagination. And by observing the people around her, and noting their idiosyncrasies and tricks of speech, she became a good character delineator.

Emily had a friend in a teacher called Mr Carpenter, and he often gave her sage counsel.

"No use trying to please everybody," he used to say. "No use trying to please critics. Live under your own hat. Don't be led away by those howls about realism. Remember pine woods are as real as pig-sties, and a darn sight pleasanter."

In L. M. Montgomery's books, and in Emily's imaginary ones, pine woods certainly triumph over pig-sties, and happy endings over sad ones. And why not? After all, in real life good often emanates from apparent evil, or, as the poet Longfellow reminds us, "celestial benedictions" are not infrequently disguised under the form of afflictions.

On the subject of happy endings Emily, like Lucy Maud, had an amusing experience. She had been requested by the editor of a publication to supply the lost portion of a story that had been running as a serial in his paper. This portion happened to be the last chapter.

A few weeks later she encountered the actual author of "The Royal Betrothal," as the serial had been called, one Mark Greaves, who called on her to complain about the ending she had given his story. He was a visitor in the town, and had seen a copy of the paper which contained Emily's version of the concluding chapter that very morning.

"I was angry—had I not a right to be?—and yet more sad than angry. My story was barbarously mutilated. *A happy ending*! Horrible. *My* ending was sorrowful and artistic. A happy ending can never be artistic."

He went on to inform her that he would teach her "the beauty and artistry of sorrow and incompleteness."

Perhaps it was at that moment that Emily remembered the advice of her mentor, Mr Carpenter, when he told her that she might just as well write about pine woods as pig-sties, since the one was as real as the other. "Sorrow and incompleteness" have been for many years the attributes of the so-called realistic or modern school of fiction, which is still so much in vogue. And pig-sties flourish in abundance in most of it. But Emily had already made her choice. Like Lucy Maud, she shared with the romanticists of all times a genuine love for a real story, with "a beginning, a middle, and an ending." She liked also to depict the triumph of good over evil, even though the triumph had to be sometimes on the *spiritual* rather than on the material plane.

## XX

## THE PAT BOOKS

LIFE at Norval pursued much the same pattern as that at Leaskdale. Although frequently called upon to address literary gatherings in various parts of Ontario, Lucy Maud never forgot that she was a minister's wife, and gave some of her best efforts to church and community projects. She always taught a class in Sunday School, and took an active part in the work of such societies as the Women's Auxiliary. A competent needle-woman, her sewing was in great demand. She was a designer of patterns for hand-made lace, some of which were used in magazines. At country parties she always took a piece of needle-work with her.

Another of her useful talents was her ability to play the organ. This was indeed an asset in a minister's wife, and she was often called upon to put it into practice. While at Norval she formed a dramatic club, discovering some histrionic talent in those who took part in the plays she directed.

As at Leaskdale, she employed a maid whose

assistance enabled her to continue her practice of writing in the morning, though she had the usual trouble in the matter of securing competent help. One girl, who had come out from Scotland, would insist on burning all the garbage in the kitchen stove, a practice which she continued with such tenacity of purpose that she finally had to be dismissed.

It was at Norval that two of the family pets— Pat and Good Luck—died. Daffy had parted with a long life of thirteen years at Leaskdale, as the result of a gunshot, accidental or intentional. Pat and Good Luck had singularly long lives. Good Luck lived for twenty-one years before succumbing to old age, and the other cat lived nearly as long.

Cats play a conspicuous part in most of the L. M. Montgomery books, as all lovers of her stories know, and in two of them which she completed while at Norval—*Pat of Silver Bush* and *Mistress Pat*—they are very much in evidence. As seen through the eyes of Judy, the old Irish family servant of the Pat household, they present a variety of piquant and pleasing pictures.

"Our cats be just common or garden cats, but we give thim a good home and talk to thim now and thin as inny self-respecting cat likes to be talked to, wid a bit av a compliment thrown in once in a while," says Old Judy.

An editor once told Lucy Maud that humour was her forte. Certainly her unfailing ability to see the funny side of a situation is one of her marked characteristics. The quaint sayings of Old Judy might be used to make up a calendar, with quotations for every day, that would serve to brighten existence. A week in any month might read like this:

*Sunday:* "Just be remembering, Patsy, what the Good Book says about happiness being inside av ye and not outside."

*Monday:* "It's bad luck to mate on the stairs, as the mouse said when the cat caught him half way down."

*Tuesday:* "Peculiar is he, thin? . . . I'm a bit that way mesilf. . . . Is he peculiar in being worth his salt in the way of work?"

*Wednesday:* "I always have my mirror hanging in the darkest corner of my room. . . . I know the lines are there, of course, but when they don't show plain I forget they are there."

*Thursday:* "They say he keeps twenty-five cats. Lord Master, think of it! What chanct would a poor mouse have?"

*Friday:* "I'm telling ye, the less ye do be believing the colder life do be. This bush now . . . it was nicer when it was packed full av fairies, wasn't it?"

Anne's Bedroom, Green Gables

GREEN GABLES

*Saturday:* "I've miny things to be thankful for but for nothing more than me liddle gift av seeing something to laugh at in almost iverything."

Old Judy of the Pat books is indeed a character, with a sense of values that might put to shame many of those in so-called higher walks of life. She was able to distinguish, to a surprising extent, between true and false conceptions of happiness.

"I wudn't be like ould Rob Pennock at the South Glen," she once remarked. "His wife is rale ashamed av his insibility. '*He doesn't know there's such a thing as a sunset,*' she sez to me, once, impatient like."

Old Judy, even on her death-bed, found something to laugh at. A few hours before she died she had a visitor, and she describes the event in the following words:

"There's liddle Mary now . . . she was here this afternoon wid her buttercup head shining like a star in me ould room and her liddle tongue going nineteen to the dozen. The questions she do be asking. 'Isn't there any Mrs God, Judy?' And whin I sez 'no' she did just be looking at me, and sez she solemn-like, 'Thin is God an ould bachelor, Judy?' . . . I'm thinking God Himself would ave laughed at the face av her."

I

## XXI

## IN TORONTO

IN 1934 *Anne of Green Gables* was again filmed, but this time as a 'talkie.' Hollywood's silent version of the book had not pleased L. M. Montgomery. Her chief complaint was that her beloved Prince Edward Island and Canada had been ignored, and the United States substituted for them. But in the second version the Island and Canada were given due recognition. The young actress who took the part of Anne became quite famous in the rôle, and she adopted Anne Shirley as her screen name. So whole-heartedly did she enter into the part that Lucy Maud declared, after seeing her, "There were many moments when she tricked me into feeling that she was Anne."

She did not feel so happy, however, about the other parts.

"Matthew, whom I have always seen with a long grey beard, seemed a stranger to me at first, but he was so good I finally forgot his clean-shaven face," she commented. "Marilla was not the tall, thin, austere Marilla of my conception, but it was impossible to help liking her. And Canada and the Island were given some credit for the story."

Although L. M. Montgomery had received nothing for the film rights of her first book, she made on the whole a very good income from her writing. She estimated once that her literary work had netted her at least seventy-five thousand dollars, but then, of course, she could not help thinking that, if she had used more perspicacity in the matter of handling *Anne of Green Gables*, always a best-seller, she might have earned considerably more. And there were always plenty of calls upon her money.

For some time she had been worried about the declining health of her husband. Brave man as he was, he tried heroically to fulfil the duties of his calling, but soon it became apparent that he would have to resign. This meant that the Macdonalds must leave Norval. They had many friends and ties in Toronto. Their sons were students there. Chester was by this time studying law at Osgoode Hall, while Stuart, who intended to be a doctor, was at the University of Toronto. They decided that they could not do better than settle in the city that was the hub of the publishing world in Canada and the home of many writers and artists—two types of creative workers in whom they were particularly interested.

In 1925 they took up their residence at 210A Riverside Drive in Toronto. L. M. Montgomery was already a member of the Toronto branches of the Canadian Women's Press Club and the Canadian Authors' Association. In the year that she moved to Toronto she was made an officer of the Order of the British Empire in the Honours list of King George V's Silver Jubilee in 1935. She also became a Fellow of the Royal Society of Arts and a member of the Artistes' Institute of France. Thus she was entitled to write "O.B.E." and "F.R.S.A." after her name.

In Toronto two more books came from her pen: *Anne of Windy Willows* and *Jane of Lantern Hill*. The latter book has as its locale Toronto, and some interesting sidelights are thrown on the "Queen City," whose high-water mark each year is the Canadian National Exhibition, held during the last week in August and the first one in September. Lucy Maud was fond of attending that Exhibition. A good cook, a good needlewoman, she enjoyed the exhibits of culinary skill and handiwork in the Women's Building. Once while there she stopped to examine a piece of lace which had been awarded first prize. The design was one originated by her years before, during the long winter evenings at the Cavendish farm.

*Jane of Lantern Hill*, rather a departure from her usual mode, was perhaps for this reason not given a very favourable reception by the reading public. But L. M. Montgomery, during her many years of authorship, had become as accustomed to adverse criticism as to unstinted praise. She had made a collection of the many reviews that had been published of her books. many of them highly contradictory in nature. In *Emily's Quest*, one of the trilogy so reminiscent of its author's own literary life and temperament, she describes Emily's perplexity when—after the publication of her first book—she reads the many reviews about it that express diverse points of view. A few examples from this book will serve to illustrate the nature of the commentary that was published about L. M. Montgomery's own work.

| *Favourable* | *Unfavourable* |
|---|---|
| One fancies that some of the author's characters must have been copied from real life. They are so absolutely true to nature. | [The author] never succeeds in making her characters convincing. |
| A very delightful book. | A very tiresome book. |
| On every page the work of the finished artist is apparent. | Very undistinguished fiction. |

| A book destined to live. | An ephemeral sort of affair. |
| A classic quality in the book. | A book of cheap and weak romanticism. |
| The story is a charming one, charmingly told. The characters are skilfully depicted, the dialogue deftly handled, the descriptive passages surprisingly effective. The quiet humour is delightful. | This feeble, pretentious and sentimental story—if story it can be called—is full of banalities and trivialties. |
| A unique and charming story of a rare order of literary workmanship. | A silly, worthless, colourless and desultory story. |

In the case of Emily, one of her fond relations remarked, "I would just believe only in the favourable reviews."

"Emily sighed. 'My tendency is just the other way. I can't help believing the unfavourable ones are true and that the favourable ones were written by morons.'"

And there spoke Lucy Maud herself. Once at a meeting of the Canadian Authors' Association, in the late thirties, when she had been called upon to give an address, she read a long list of "contradictory reviews" about her own work, very similar in content to those enumerated in Emily's case. It was almost as if she appealed to her audience to help her to solve a problem: which point of view was right, the favourable or the unfavourable?

All through her life there was in Lucy Maud this almost child-like credulity in regard to adverse judgments of her work. She possessed the artist's endowment of acute sensitivity, and it would be idle to contend that she was not hurt by the 'slings and arrows' of those who did not like her books. Fortunately, these were relatively few. Time brought her the philosophic outlook. She came to realize that, just as in life there are "those that love us and those that hate us" (as the Prayer Book has it), so in literature people have their sometimes antithetical tastes. As for those whose dislike, due to jealousy or emulation, takes the form of active enmity, she has this to say in one of her poems in *The Watchman*, entitled "To My Enemy":

> *Thanks, endless thanks, to thee I owe*
> *For that my lifelong journey through*
> *Thine honest hate has done for me*
> *What love perchance had failed to do.*
>
> *Thine anger struck from me a fire*
> *That purged all dull content away.*
> *Our mortal strife to me has been*
> *Unflagging spur from day to day.*

*And thus, while all the world may laud*
*The gifts of love and loyalty,*
*I lay my meed of gratitude*
*Before thy feet, mine enemy!*

## XXII

## LAST YEARS

WITH the outbreak of the Second World War in 1939 a change began to take place in the bright and buoyant bearing of L. M. Montgomery. She tired easily, and her friends noticed that at times she was very nervous.

"At some of our Women's Press Club meetings, I thought she looked far from well, and I was distressed to see how white she was and how her hands shook," said Mrs Donald MacGregor (Marian Keith), in describing her impressions of the state of her friend's health during the last two years of her life.

A lover of the gentler courses of life, in which art and beauty have a chance to flourish, L. M Montgomery witnessed with dismay the advent of a period of martial austerity, inimical to all the values she cherished, ushered in by the War. Then, too, her husband's ill health contributed to her anxieties. He who had played so manly a part in the rôles of minister, husband, and father was now utterly dependent upon her. For the first time, after more than thirty-five years of continuous literary output, she had no desire to write more, and she felt with the poet that the "time past" of her life must suffice her.

During the winter of 1942 she compiled a collection of magazine stories she had written many years before. Among these were the ones that had been 'lost' for a time, pending the termination of her lawsuit against the Boston publisher who had used them without her authorization. Under the title of *Further Chronicles of Avonlea* she placed the collection of stories in the hands of a publisher.

This book of stories, which had been 'lost' for over thirty years, she was destined never to see in its final form. Nor did she see the first Canadian edition of her books which came off the press in 1942. It was on Friday, April 24 of that year—the very day on which she had placed *Further Chronicles of Avonlea* with a publisher—that she succumbed to the insidious illness that had undermined her strength for so many months. A writer of stories whose appeal was to the young in heart of all ages had come to her journey's end.

It is fitting that her resting-place should be in that island whose red soil, green fields, and sea she had so much loved, and had immortalized in fiction—her native province of Prince Edward Island. The funeral took place at Cavendish, and, as her old friend Fanny Wise (Mrs R. E. Mutch, of Charlottetown) expressed it, "a path was beaten to her grave." She is buried in a graveyard on a hill overlooking Green Gables

> *. . . where the meadows wide*
> *Greenly lie on every side,*
> *And the murmur of the sea*
> *Comes across the orient lea.*

Later a memorial service was held for her.

"It took place on a hot day in August," related Mrs Mutch, "and there were long prayers and long Presbyterian hymns. Two women fainted."

And then she went on to describe the impressiveness of the occasion. People who had loved L. M. Montgomery and her work came by the thousands, not only from the hamlets, villages, towns and cities of Prince Edward Island, but from far places in the Maritime Provinces, Ontario, Quebec, and the United States. The roads leading to Cavendish were choked with cars and buses, and the Gulf of St Lawrence was vocal with the sound of motor launches that brought fishermen and their families to the scene.

"Yes, she was well loved in her life, and in death she will not be forgotten," declared Mrs Mutch.

A year later the Rev. Ewan Macdonald, who

had for so long been ill, died, and his grave is beside that of his wife. And so two natives of Prince Edward Island came home at the last.

Every summer at Cavendish hundreds of people from all parts of Canada, the United States and other countries join in paying tribute to the memory of L. M. Montgomery. There is a big stone monument to her near the entrance of the Cavendish National Park, but it is not needed to remind her friends that such an original and lovable human being once lived among them. Her best monument is her work. It is still a vitalizing force and a source of inspiration to those of all ages who are in heart 'for ever young.'

## PUBLISHER'S POSTSCRIPT

THIS brief story of a woman who has given so much pleasure to others takes little account of the commercial success that attended L. M. Montgomery's work, and none at all of the impact that she made upon millions of people living outside the Americas.

*Anne of Green Gables* was first brought to England by Sir Isaac Pitman and Sons, Ltd, in 1908; *Anne of Avonlea* followed in 1909, *Kilmeny of the Orchard* in 1910, *The Story Girl* in 1911, and *Anne of the Island* in 1915.

Although nine thousand copies of *Anne of Green Gables* were sold in the first three years, the public interest in the Montgomery books progressively diminished to vanishing-point, until by 1919 all of the first four titles were out of print. *Anne of the Island*, published in 1915, did not succeed in reviving the demand for the earlier books, and, indeed, was itself a publishing failure at that time.

From 1921 to 1933 Hodder and Stoughton, Ltd, published some of the later books, starting with *Rilla of Ingleside* and following with *Emily of New Moon*, *Emily Climbs*, *The Blue Castle*,

*Emily's Quest*, *Magic for Marigold*, and finally *Pat of Silver Bush*, but although they sold over a hundred thousand copies of these titles, the "Anne Books," as they are now universally called, lay dormant until, in 1924, L. C. Page and Co., of Boston, entered into a contract simultaneously with George G. Harrap and Co., Ltd, of London, and Angus and Robertson, Ltd, of Sydney, Australia, for the republication of all the books that they controlled.

This appears to have been the turning-point in L. M. Montgomery's climb to fame in Britain and Australia, for the public at once showed a renewed interest in her work, and to-day, to say nothing of the men-folk, there are millions of grandmothers, mothers, aunts, daughters, and nieces who have been brought up with Anne, and who are happier for having met her and many other interesting characters created by Lucy Maud in her books.

Of the three million Montgomery novels circulated in the British Commonwealth, excluding Canada, since 1925 more than six hundred thousand copies of *Anne of Green Gables* alone have been sold, and of these nearly a quarter of a million have been bought in Australia and New Zealand. With the present population of those two countries approximately eleven million (of which many are infants and "New Australians," who have not yet mastered their new language), and taking into account that every book in circulation has many readers, this achievement is truly remarkable.

Anne's popularity has now gone far beyond the English-speaking peoples, and the influence of her lovable personality may soon be more widely felt in Africa, where *Anne of Green Gables* has recently been adopted for use in one of the large Native Training Colleges.

W.G.H.